My Wonderful Life
… being in the right place at the right time

by
Rene A. Henry

© 2016, Gollywobbler Productions

LIBRARY OF CONGRESS CATALOGING-IN-PUBLICATION DATA
Henry, Rene A. (1933-   )

My Wonderful Life … being in the right place at the right time
Rene A. Henry – 1st ed.
      p.   cm.
Includes biographical references and index
ISBN# 978-0-9674535-6-9
1. Rene A. Henry. 2. Autobiography. 3. Business.
4. Public Relations. 5. The College of William & Mary.
6. Olympics. 7. Sports. 8. West Virginia University
I. Title

Library of Congress Control Number: 2015903764

© 2016, Rene A. Henry
Gollywobbler Productions
1474 21st Avenue
Seattle, Washington 98122
www.renehenry.com

Cover design by Jack Cullimore
Jack Cullimore Graphic Design, Ilwaco, Washington
Cover photograph courtesy of The College of William & Mary
Alumni Association

All rights reserved. No part of this book may be reproduced or transmitted in any form or by any means, electrical or mechanical, including photocopying, recording, or by any information storage and retrieval system without permission in writing from the copyright owner.

First Edition, 2016
10 9 8 7 6 5 4 3 2 1
Printed in the United States of America

Foreword

I wrote this book primarily for my children and granddaughter, family and close friends. Several former business associates have been pushing me for years to write a book about my career and outline some of my practices, philosophies and strategies that could be of benefit and interest to others.

Several years ago Harvey Posert, my good friend for more than 50 years, first suggested I write this book and cite some of my successes and interesting experiences. Just a month weeks before he passed away he asked when I was going to finish writing this book. I thank him for his persistence in making this possible. I told Harvey I didn't know who would want to read a book of my memoires, much less buy a copy. Only time will tell.

I hope readers will enjoy my book and practitioners of all ages may find one helpful idea that worked for me.

— Rene A. Henry
September 15, 2016

Chapter 1

How It All Began

Psychologists and behavior scientists believe that our formative years are critical for development, performance and success throughout life. Some experts say that the first five years are the most important while others believe the years from either birth to eight or even as long as 12 years old are the most important.

I was born June 13, 1933 in Charleston, West Virginia during the post-depression era. Charleston is the state's capital and then had a population of about 75,000. It was the chemical center of the world and fumes and emissions of every type were in the air all throughout the Kanawha Valley. I wonder what waste was also dumped into the rivers. Throughout the years little has changed. I believe the state has always made corporate profit and the economy a priority over the environment and public health.

Growing up I never could have dreamed that someday I would meet and even spend time with five presidents of the United States[1], the heads of state of several foreign countries[2], dozens of governors, mayors and members of Congress, and also know and work with scores of sports superstars and Hollywood movie and television actors.

---
1 Richard M. Nixon, Gerald R. Ford, Ronald Reagan, George H. W. Bush, George W. Bush.
2 Jean Chrétien, Canada; Said Musa, Belize; Valdas Adamkus, Lithuania.

I was fortunate to have a diversified professional career that I attribute to my liberal arts education at William & Mary. Sports, journalism, and public relations have been a part of my life as long as I can remember. Additionally, I had careers in higher education; housing, real estate and construction; television and entertainment; association management; federal service; and even politics.

My father was the youngest of three sons of my grandparents who came to the U.S. from Belgium before the turn of the century. They were among the first families to settle South Charleston, West Virginia before spending time in Charleroi, Pennsylvania and Sheridan, Indiana. My grandfather was a Belgian glassworker from Jumet and a member of a glass making cooperative. He anglicized his name from Francois Henri to Frank Henry, so when my father was born he was named Rene, without the French accent René, which is why my given name has no accent.

My grandfather hand made all of the window glass in their house. Later in the early 1900s my grandparents built South Charleston's first brick building that is still standing and in use today. In it they opened a news, magazine and confectionery store. It was here my father was poisoned by gas while working to repair a broken refrigeration line. He caught pneumonia and died two days later, just several months before my fifth birthday. Over the years I somehow dropped the "Jr." from my name which I now regret. In the preceding year I lost both grandfather Henry and my maternal grandmother, Clara Bell Jarrett Reveal.

My mother and I lived with her father, C. O. Reveal, a retired railroad conductor we all affectionately called Daddy Oat. I traced my mother's side of the family to living in West Virginia back as far as 1850. She worked at two jobs – playing the piano at Galperin's music store in the department where people bought sheet music and at Elizabeth Embleton's dance school. Often on weekends she would play piano for a dance band. As a teenager she even played the organ for silent movies and for most of her life was a church organist. While growing up I spent a great deal of time with my grandmother, Marie Josephine Brichaux Henry.

2 | My Wonderful Life

During the summers we visited my aunt Hazel and uncle Lucius Exley and my cousin Dot on Long Island. In 1940 when they lived in Glenwood Landing there was a polio epidemic in Charleston and my mother believed it was safest for me live with them for several months. It was a traumatic experience for me. I was in a new school, I had no friends, my father had passed away two years earlier and I didn't know when I would see those I was closest to – my mother, grandfather and grandmother. I really missed my dog, a collie named Duke. He was my best friend and would walk me to school in the morning and was always there to walk me home in the afternoon. Once he protected me from three older bullies. I finished the first half of second grade in New York and when it was safe to return home in December my elementary school advanced me a grade. The worst was that Duke was gone. The bullies he protected me from taunted him and he bit one. My grandfather placed him with friends on a farm.

It was at the Exley home where my mother married William K. Secrest when I was nine years old. I was fortunate to have a wonderful and loving step-father I called Bill. He worked in freight sales for the New York Central Railroad and his father, whom we called Pop, lived with us. He was a retired railroad locomotive engineer.

There was always a Baldwin baby grand piano in our home and I wish I had learned how to play the piano. Instead, in the second grade I began taking clarinet lessons and played for the next seven years. I was never destined to be another Benny Goodman or Artie Shaw. I very much regret that I never learned French from all the time I spent with my grandmother.

The First Step to Writing

During my pre-teen and early teenage years I spent a lot of time in a printing company owned by my aunt and uncle, Jewell and Bill Jones. Here I learned how to set type by hand by taking small individual pieces of metal type from a job case – a large box with 89 individual compartments for letters, numbers and symbols – and

How It All Began | 3

placing them one at a time upside down and backwards in a composing stick. After several lines of type had been composed I tied the type together with a string and transferred it to a galley and when placed in a metal chase locked it in place. You had to remember all of the compartments not just to compose what was to be printed but also to return the movable type to its proper place in the case when the job was printed.

I also learned how to operate a hand fed platen press and was on my way to becoming a young apprentice in the industry. I could well have worked at Jones Printing Co. when I graduated from high school.

When I was in the seventh grade my Christmas present was a new Remington portable typewriter. My step-father saw me "hunt-and-peck" typing so he got me a typing text book and black tabs to cover the keys. He motivated me to learn to touch type. I practiced every day and taught myself how to type. This has been a tremendous value to me all my life. I believe the years of playing clarinet contributed to my finger dexterity. During my U.S. Army induction tests I typed 96 words a minute on a manual typewriter. An officer thought I cheated and made me retake the test. After 30 seconds of typing, a captain said "the score is correct." I have typed 120 words a minute or faster on an electric. For years my writing thinking process has been through my fingers.

I'm not sure when I first started writing – perhaps it was in the seventh grade in junior high school. I wrote sports and reported on events for the Roosevelt Junior High School *Torch*. I also phoned in game results to the local *Charleston Gazette*, often talking to the sports editor, Shorty Hardman.

My good friend, Howard Kight, suggested we write for a weekly newspaper in South Charleston. My grandmother knew the editor of *The Free Press* and he gave us the opportunity. He paid us five cents a word for any story he printed which did not encourage us to be brief and to the point. I continued as a contributing writer to the newspaper through much of high school.

I was active in the Cub Scouts and then the Boy Scouts well

into high school until there were too many demands on my time. If I had it to do over again I would have learned Morse code instead of becoming proficient at semaphore, the use of flag telegraphy. Perhaps it was the influence of the U.S. Navy when we lived in Norfolk, Va.

A Decision – Music or Journalism

When I started the tenth grade, Bill Secrest was promoted to head the New York Central's office in Norfolk, Virginia. Here my career began to blossom. At my new Granby High School I had to choose between the band and being on the newspaper since both were at the same time. Russell Williams, the band director, made the decision for me telling me I needed more lessons before I could play in the Granby band even though for the previous three years in Charleston I was in the first chair clarinet section of the all-city band. I thanked him for his decision years later at a school reunion.

I was in the right place at the right time because the school newspaper needed a sports editor. In each of the following two years I won first place in Virginia for sports story writing by the honorary Quill & Scroll Society, judged at Northwestern's Medill School of Journalism.

During the fall of 1949, Mark Scott, the sports director of Norfolk's leading sports-news-music station asked the local high school sports editors to call him with daily reports on the various athletic teams. Again, I was in the right place at the right time. He was impressed with my responsiveness and thoroughness and invited me to the radio station which led to a part-time job. Working in radio sports was a wonderful experience. During the summer I would be with Scott and Erik Paige in the press box when they broadcast the home games of the Norfolk Tars minor league baseball team. They also reconstructed New York Yankees baseball games, receiving information from a Western Union telegraph operator who sat in one corner of the studio.

During the fall WNOR was the originating radio station for the Tobacco States Football Network. I became part of their team and traveled to colleges in Virginia and North Carolina every Saturday to broadcast football games. I got to know the sports information directors and several even recruited me for jobs at their colleges.

One day the radio station news director received a call from the United Press bureau chief in Richmond. He asked me if I wanted to cover a professional golf tournament at Virginia Beach for UPI. I was the only one at the station willing to work for such little pay. But more important I was in the right place at the right time. This led to dozens of other UPI assignments and to my writing a weekly column about Virginia high school sports.

In my senior year I learned that if you really want something, you have to go for it. Every year the seniors voted for classmates in six categories that included "Most Athletic," "Most Intellectual," "Most Popular," and "Most Valuable." The winners were photographed for a full page in the yearbook. A committee chose two boys and girls for each category and names were not announced until the vote so there was no campaigning. One morning in homeroom we were asked to vote and I was surprised my name was a finalist for "Most Valuable." I had always been taught to support the other person. Votes were tallied by homerooms. I voted for my opponent. He voted for himself. If I had abstained it would have been a tie. If I had voted for myself, I would have won. It was a lesson I learned to always believe in yourself.

Next Stop – Williamsburg, Virginia

I worked with Erik Paige when he broadcast the William & Mary basketball games. I graduated in January 1951 and rather than wait until the fall to start college at one of several I had on my short list, I decided to enroll at William & Mary, albeit late. I began my first classes in the third week of the new semester. I needed to re-acclimate to study and by the time I saw my mid-term grades – two Ds, two Fs and a B – I wondered if I would be in college in June. I was and passed all of the courses with Cs or better and went on to major in economics.

Starting with the fall semester I had two part-time jobs. I

worked in the sports information office as assistant to the sports information director and also became a student assistant to Dudley Jensen, the director of intramural sports. Two summers I took classes to enable me to graduate in three-and-one-half years. One summer I sold programs to the play *Common Glory* at the college's outdoor amphitheater.

On the William & Mary campus we were immersed in our nation's history with the college's contributions, priorities, traditions and buildings. However, I never really appreciated all of the historic surroundings of Colonial Williamsburg until after I graduated and returned for vacations. Exceptions were the low student green fees at the Williamsburg Inn's golf course and beers with classmates at Chowning's Tavern.

My parents now lived in Virginia Beach and one summer I worked at the popular Surf Club on the ocean beachfront. During the day I did office work and gave swimming lessons and in the evening had a variety of assignments that included wearing a white dinner jacket. The big bands and vocalists of the era performed at the club – Stan Kenton with Maynard Ferguson, Buddy Rich, Mel Torme, Louis Prima, Ted Straeter, and others. After day work I would often swim out past the breakers and then parallel to the beach for up to a half mile or so and then jog back on the sand. Next it was home for dinner and to change for the evening.

Our home was on the Princess Anne Country Club Golf Course with the dogleg 10th fairway in our backyard and the 17th green directly across the street. By the time I got home no one was playing and I could always get in an easy eight holes of golf. There were no fences around homes and the gentlemen and lady golfers in those days would never wander into someone's back yard to retrieve a ball hit out of bounds. Thanks to my step-grandfather Pop, I never had to buy a golf ball and always had a bucket of nearly new ones to play with.

A Career Jump Start

In February 1953 I was again in the right place at the right time. Sam Banks, who had been my boss as the sports information director, left to head public relations for the Baltimore Colts professional football team. Jack Freeman, the athletic director and head football coach, offered me his job and gave me a $10 a month raise to $60. This jump- started my professional career. The job was considered a full-time job and I was carrying an 18-hour course load; was an officer in Sigma Nu fraternity; continued my job in intramural sports; competed in intramural sports; and ran the high and low hurdles on the varsity track team. I surprised myself academically finishing with four Cs and two Bs. I took three summer school courses that relieved some academic pressure for my senior year and two A's increased my grade point average.

I had no one to tell me how best to do my job and it was on-the-job learning. I sought information from my counterparts at other colleges who were all older full-time professionals. I had a very limited budget and I hired classmates for 50 cents an hour to help me mimeograph, fold and mail news releases. One evening as we prepared a mailing Marshall Ries asked why, if the news was important, we were sending it second class mail. I said it was my limited budget. He responded, "It only costs a penny more to go first class." Freeman was working late in his office and obviously heard that because the next day he told me to mail everything first class.

I had no budget to hire professional photographers. My love for photography started one pre-teen Christmas when I received two Kodak Brownie cameras as gifts. By the time I was in junior high school I even developed the 127 film and made contact prints because I could not afford an enlarger. In high school I upgraded to a 35mm camera.

The athletic department had a professional 4x5 Speed Graphic camera I used to photograph players on the football and basketball teams. I used a lab on campus to do the processing and make prints for the media. We also had a 16mm Bell & Howell tri-turret movie camera I used to produce a 30-minute film about the college for recruiting purposes. Dr. Al Haak, a fine arts professor, who helped me with the editing, did the narration. All of this would be most helpful to me in years to come.

As the years passed I became more proficient with my photography and even won competitive prizes given by newspapers. When a San Francisco camera store heard from professional photographer friends about photographs I had taken at the 1962 Seattle World's Fair they created an exhibit of mine in their street window showcase.

The same month Freeman named me sports information director there was a violation of the college's Honor Code that decimated the football team to only 24 players. The 1953 team had a remarkable season losing only once in its first six games and finished with a 5-4-1 record. It became known as "The Iron Indians" with wins over Wake Forest, Virginia Tech, North Carolina State, Richmond, George Washington and a tie against a then nationally-ranked Navy. It was a feat that will never again be repeated by another college football team. This prompted my writing the book and a motion picture screenplay titled *The Iron Indians*.

By springtime in my senior year I was being recruited by other colleges and universities. Again, I was in the right place at the right time. I decided on West Virginia University even though others offered higher salaries. For someone in the public relations business, I believed WVU could be a dream job. And, it was.

Chapter 2

Returning Home To West Virginia

Growing up in Charleston I had never been to Morgantown or West Virginia University. My first time was when William & Mary played in the 1955 Southern Conference basketball tournament. I sat at press row and also covered the tournament for the *Newport News Daily Press*. Sitting next to me at the end of the press table was Hot Rod Hundley who had just finished an incredible freshman year for the Mountaineers. Little did I know then that several months later I would be promoting him for All-American honors and that first meeting was the beginning of our life-long friendship.

Everyone at WVU went out of their way to welcome and recruit me for the sports information director job. The football coach, Art "Pappy" Lewis came by daily to give me a sales pitch. I was in the right place at the right time and made the right decision choosing WVU even though it was only for a two-year, interim appointment and the salary was well below other job opportunities at comparable universities. I filled in for Edgar O. "Eddie" Barrett while he was on active-duty in the U.S. Air Force.

In addition to Hundley, my new job was the start of other lifelong friendships that included Barrett, basketball coach Fred

Schaus and players Jerry West, Pete White, Paul Witting and Joedy Gardner and football stars Sam Huff, Fred Wyant, Gary Bunn and Gene "Beef" Lamone. Schaus, Hundley, West and I reunited in Los Angeles when they were with the Los Angeles Lakers.

I was fortunate to be sports information director during two of the Mountaineers greatest years in sports. There was little job pressure during the summer months so I took graduate courses in the business school and played a lot of golf that included several trips to The Greenbrier in White Sulphur Springs with WVU sports teams.

Shorty Hardman, sports editor of *The Charleston Gazette*, who only a few years earlier I called with junior high school game results, became a good friend. I also listened to WVU basketball games broadcast by Jack Fleming, for decades the "Voice of the Mountaineers." Jack and I became lifelong friends as did Hardman, Mickey Furfari, the sports editor of the Morgantown *Dominion-News* and William Dent "Bill" Evans, editor of *The Fairmont Times*.

A First for Sports and Higher-Education

In the mid-1950s, sports information directors sent glossy, black-and-white photographs of key players not only to newspapers but to television stations. The use of video news releases, or VNRs, was in its infancy. Wikipedia reports the extensive use of VNRs in the 1980s, nearly three decades later. Then SIDs were expected to be in the city of an away football game by mid-week to help promote the game. I didn't have the luxury of a staff or budget to do that and instead sent short 16mm film features to the TV stations. I don't know when we started calling them VNRs.

During 1955 spring football practice I filmed players to incorporate into game action footage. The difficult task was reviewing the game films using a standard 16mm Bell & Howell projector and a home movie editor/splicer. We had no professional equipment on campus. Being able to use a Movieola, at which I became very adept 20 years later, would have been a dream.

I combined the game excerpts with the staged footage and

created four 60-to-90-second VNRs that featured several All-American candidates. Jack Fleming did the narration over music of the Mountaineer fight song. I sent the four masters to a film lab in Pittsburgh and four copies of each were produced. I then cut the masters apart and respliced segments back into the game film. The entire project cost less than $200.

I sent these pioneer VNRs to television stations to promote the team and players. I sent the station a script so an announcer could do his own voice-over or use our sound track. With our limited budget I asked the stations to please return the VNRs so I could bicycle them to others.

This was so successful that I produced a three-minute B-roll of basketball game action showing Hot Rod Hundley making incredible shots, passes and clowning. Before our first game in New York City the incredible Jim McKay used the clip in is entirety during the five minutes he was allocated to give viewers sports on WCBS-TV.

It was years before anyone in sports and even in higher education used VNRs as a public relations tool. This project would be simple today with the digital technology available. In 1956 I also produced the first college Spring Football Media Guide.

In my two wonderful years promoting WVU sports, Hundley was first team All-American and in football Sam Huff and Bruce Bosley, both tackles, were consensus All-American. Many others were honored at various levels. My portfolio was filled with clippings that included major stories in *Life* magazine, a half dozen in *Sports Illustrated*, and spreads in *Look, Time, Collier's* and scores of major newspapers.

Mad Men the Way It Was

When Eddie Barrett returned it was time for me to move on. Athletic Director Robert N. "Red" Brown, my boss, encouraged me to look to New York and in a field other than sports. "You can always have a job in sports anytime you want," he told me. Much has changed in public relations, advertising, and media since I got into the business. In 1956, I decided to make the move from sports to Madison

Avenue where I encountered my first signs of discrimination.

The *New York Times* classified section had pages of display advertising for jobs. However, many I wanted to seek had a bold face listing at the bottom of the ad – **Ivy Only**. If you didn't have a degree from one of the eight Ivy League universities your chances of getting a job were nil. When you walked into the reception room, one of the first things you would see on the receptionist's desk was an "Ivy Only" plaque. She was not allowed to take your résumé and human resources would not grant an interview unless you graduated from Brown, Columbia, Cornell, Dartmouth, Harvard, Princeton, Penn or Yale.

The same was true for much of the publishing industry. Ivies were preferred at all of the Time, Inc. magazines. Depending on the job, the radio and TV networks – ABC, CBS and NBC – were much more liberal and where I had opportunities to stay in sports.

The award-winning television series *Mad Men* portrayed things the way they were. It was even more difficult for women. The only Madison Avenue jobs for women were as a secretary, clerk/typist or receptionist. Applicants not only had to be graduates of one of the "Seven Sisters," the women's Ivies – Barnard, Bryn Mawr, Mount Holyoke, Radcliffe, Smith, Vassar, and Wellesley – but also Katherine Gibbs, a New York City business school that specialized in typing and secretarial skills.

The only other way to get inside the door for an interview or even talk with someone was through a personal or networking contact. A number of non-Ivies did work on Madison Avenue and there were opportunities if you had the connections.

After two weeks of pounding the streets of Manhattan, I returned to Morgantown discouraged and to plan my next move. Then I had a call from an executive search firm. Owens-Corning Fiberglas wanted to hire me for its public relations agency in Toledo, Ohio. Within two weeks I was on my way as a young account executive at Flournoy & Gibbs, a prestigious firm that represented a score of blue chip clients.

From sports I soon turned to selling issues, products and

services. While I spent most of my professional career in public relations I never took a course in PR or journalism. My liberal arts education at William & Mary, combined with on-the-job training, prepared me well with essential fundamentals and disciplines and contributed significantly to my success in diverse management positions I held.

My new job was interrupted in October with a call from the U.S. Army. Following basic training at Ft. Chaffee, Arkansas, I was assigned to the press office at Aberdeen Proving Ground, Maryland, where I also played on the post's basketball, tennis and swim teams and coached track. I was named assistant coach of the 2nd Army track team. During the All-Army Championships at Ft. Hood, Texas I reunited with Rod Hundley where he was in basic training. His military career did not last long because of two bad knees that required surgery several years before. He soon was playing with the Lakers.

A Return to Sports

By mid-summer I was back in sports information assigned to the athletic department at the U.S. Military Academy at West Point. I reconnected with and expanded my media contacts. I did a number of tasks including writing the football programs for the Notre Dame and Navy games and scouted Army's basketball opponents. I became friends with sportscaster Mel Allen who broadcast Army's football games on radio. I could not have survived financially on the $63 a month salary of a private first class but Lester Scott, who ran the press office at Madison Square Garden, gave me free-lance assignments for Knicks and college games for several newspapers. I was in New York City four nights of the week and remember seeing more than 120 basketball games that year. I reconnected again with Rod Hundley and following a Knicks game against the Minneapolis Lakers on New Year's Eve, I walked to Times Square with him and Coach George Mikan and stood protected and flanked by them as we watched the ball drop down to welcome in 1958. I spent weekends visiting college friends and fraternity brothers – Gil Parmele on Staten Island, Pete Kalison in Manhattan and Marshall Ries in Queens. Sometimes I would stay with my cousin Dot and her husband Dave Erickson in Lincoln Park, New Jersey.

I knew all of New York's leading sportswriters. I "hung out" with a young Jimmy Breslin and often had drinks with him and celebrities at Toots Shor's. I saw every home football game of the New York Giants in 1957 and even had press parking and access credentials to the tennis championships at Forest Hills.

Revisiting Stony Brook

In high school I continued to spend summers with my aunt Hazel and uncle Lucius Exley and cousin Dot. When they lived in Stony Brook on Long Island's North Shore I met Gillian Thompson who several years later would become my wife. When I was on active duty at West Point we renewed an earlier romance and were married in September 1958 after my honorable discharge from active military service. She had worked in San Francisco the previous year and when I returned to my old job she soon found that Toledo was no comparison to where she had been living and suggested we move there.

When I returned to Flournoy & Gibbs, my sports experience was beneficial for our client AP Parts whose race car was going for an unprecedented third straight win in the Indianapolis 500. No Indy car before had the national pre-race exposure that I generated. Arrangements were made to ship the car to New York to be on *The Ed Sullivan Show* if it won. The driver and car had the fastest qualifying time and the #1 pole position for the race. However, when the race official announced, "Gentlemen, start your engines" the car wouldn't start and it was pushed off the track.

My first taste of Hollywood was working on a Toledo homecoming for Danny Thomas and fund raising event for St. Jude's Hospital. As a young account executive, I was assigned to assist him in any way while he was in town. His popular TV show at the time was *Make Room for Daddy*.

I began a direct-mail campaign to seek a job in San Francisco. In August 1959 I was hired by Lennen & Newell, then the tenth largest advertising agency in the world. I was in the right place at the right time. Robert G. Williams, the senior vice president and account supervisor for the Simpson Timber Company account liked the work I had done for Owens-Corning and my experience in the home building industry.

In the days before jets, I left Toledo after work on Friday, flew to California, had the interview Saturday, was hired, flew back Sunday and gave notice on Monday. California here we come!

Chapter 3

Open Your Golden Gates

When I told a colleague at Flournoy & Gibbs that I was moving to San Francisco he looked at me with his mouth open and said: "My God... that's in California!" Indeed it is. Until then I had lived no farther west than Toledo. It was a big move for me but I trusted my wife that we would love living there. And we did. It also was a challenge because many of my media contacts were in New York City.

San Francisco was incredible in the Sixties. It was like no other city in the U.S. All of the women wore gloves and hats. The St. Francis Hotel even had a man working full time polishing coins so women's gloves would not get dirty. Taxi drivers even got out to open the passenger door for a woman.

Dining was elegant at Ernie's with hosts-owners Roland and Victor Gotti and at Alexis with maitre d' André. A jacket and tie was required at most restaurants. There are photos of this era with men in suits, ties and hats riding on the cable cars. My favorite Italian restaurant was Fior d'Italia which had been owned by the Marianetti family since 1886. For lunch my business colleagues and I would often walk to Chinatown or to North Beach for a Joe's Special. Many Italian restaurants served lunch family style. A treat would be a Shrimp Louie in the Garden Court of the Palace Hotel or fresh cracked Dungeness crab and sourdough bread at Fisherman's Wharf.

Another favorite was Schroeder's where you never knew who would be seated with you at large round tables. Women were not allowed for lunch and had to be escorted for dinner. I am sure that has long since changed. Doro's was a luncheon choice when hosting a client. The Kingston Trio and the Smothers Brothers frequented the Hungry i. and Phyllis Diller and Mort Sahl were regulars at the Purple Onion. For cocktails there was the Top of the Mark or the Tonga Room or Crown Room at The Fairmont.

When you opened the *San Francisco Chronicle*, you turned first to read Herb Caen's column. Every PR man strived to get his client in print. It helped being friends with Caen's assistant, Jerry Bundsen. The skyline was the same as it had been for years. Driving from Oakland across the Bay Bridge you could see the cable cars going up and down California Street. The first four years we lived in the Marina District one block from Marina Green and the Bay. After Deborah was born we moved to Marin County where Bruce was born two years later. It was an experience every day driving up the Waldo Grade past Sausalito and emerging from the tunnel to always see a different and glorious site of San Francisco – sometimes shrouded in fog or the morning sun glistening on the towers of the Golden Gate Bridge.

A Great Mentor

I was fortunate to have a boss who took me under his wing. Robert G. Williams was the number two person in the Lennen & Newell San Francisco office and a wonderful mentor. L&N then was the tenth largest advertising agency in the world and had branch offices in San Francisco, with 75 employees, and Los Angeles, with 25. This was during the era of mergers and acquisitions and the firm was private and independent.

Writer and author Jack Finney took a break looking for new material and was one of our copywriters. That's where he got the idea and characters for his successful book and movie, *Good Neighbor Sam*. Simpson Timber Company was my primary account and gave me my introduction to Seattle where it was headquartered. Some

40 years later it would become my home.

Another client was Paramount Pictures and everyone included San Francisco on any movie promotion tour. This meant taking care of numerous celebrities that included Joseph E. Levine, Jill St. John, Edith Head, Otto Preminger, Marty Allen and Steve Rossi, Jack Jones, and Kim Novak. Client meetings in Los Angeles always included lunch in the famous Studio Commissary. One was with Cornel Wilde who was preparing to direct and star in *The Naked Prey* in Africa and asked my help to get recording equipment donated.

Just before my 30th birthday I was fortunate to be named "Public Relations Man of the Year" by the San Francisco Bay Area Publicity Club. When our office of L&N merged with a prominent local agency, Bob Williams left to open his own small boutique agency. I knew then it was time for a career move and for the first time in nearly 10 years I prepared a résumé.

Through parents' get-togethers at a pre-school in Marin County I became friends with Harvey Posert who ran the San Francisco office for Daniel J. Edelman. I knew Dan through meetings of associations he represented where my clients were members. In December 1967 I became a vice president and opened the Edelman office in Los Angeles which I headed for the next four years.

Oooh LA LA

Once more being in the right place at the right time, I was heading south and taking a major step in my professional career. I located our office on Wilshire Blvd. near the corner of Westwood Blvd. Within three months we were serving clients that included 3M, Sunkist and a new organization of the nation's 11 largest home builders and community developers: the Council of Housing Producers. The office immediately operated in the black, I added staff as we grew, and it was profitable every year until I left in December 1970 to start my own business.

Dan and I spoke almost daily. I learned marketing PR from him, much about strategies to develop new business, and especially client relations. When we retained new business Dan would always call the office head one month later and ask for a report on what had been done for the client. This is truly customer service and something PR executives today should practice and clients should demand. I talked weekly with Harvey Posert in San Francisco and Robert J. "Bob" Stone in our New York office.

Several months into the job Harold Burson called. He wanted me to head his Los Angeles office of Burson-Marsteller. He offered me a salary half again more than what I was making and said he would reimburse Edelman for all expenses involved. I told him I made a commitment to both Dan and my clients and didn't believe it would be either ethical or professional to leave. That was the beginning of a long friendship with Harold.

As the office continued to profit and grow we moved to Century City and soon had a staff of 13. Before it was called sports marketing we were extensively involved working with Sunkist that included sponsorships and site signage at sports events.

For a number of its association clients, Edelman served double duty handling administration and serving as the executive director. I did this for the Council of Housing Producers that grew to 15 members. The presidents and CEOs represented their companies. Some were publicly held, some private and others a division of a public company. I worked Wall Street and the halls of Congress to stress the difference of these home builders in contrast to the average, small American builder. Media always called me for input when doing a story on the industry. As a first, I began organizing meetings for the financial community in major cities with all members participating. Two records were set for a luncheon meeting of the New York Society of Security Analysts – the largest attendance and the first time companies not publicly held were on a program. The Council established record audiences as well in Los Angeles, Chicago and Houston.

The firm's largest account was the Wine Institute, the producers of California wine. Harvey ran it from San Francisco and my responsibility in Los Angeles was to provide California wines to be seen in movies and on television and to create celebrity wine tasting events. Vincent Price was our spokesperson and I met with him regularly. At one wine tasting at his Bel Air home I met Jack Lemmon, Art Linkletter, Ozzie and Harriett Nelson and Betty White. I worked with Glenn Ford to host a tasting at his home. Through Shelly Saltman, a close friend from sports days, Jerry Perenchio hosted a tasting honoring Andy Williams. Through other contacts I became friends with Karl Malden and Don Drysdale who were always on my invitation lists.

I thoroughly enjoyed my relationship with Dan and his organization and was often approached by executive search firms to move. A former client that was a conflict with an Edelman client needed my help and suggested I resign, start my own business and handle their business. It was too good an offer to turn down. I was in the right place at the right time.

Dan Edelman paid me a wonderful compliment in his biography when the author wrote: *When Henry left to form his own agency in 1970, Dan attempted to replace him with a series of experienced managers culled from other Edelman offices. None of them succeeded to Dan's satisfaction. ... [T]he office struggled to stay in business and on the verge of closing in 1978.*

My Own Business

In January 1971, I launched Rene A. Henry, Inc., with the Asphalt Roofing Manufacturers' Association as my first client. Sunkist and the Council of Housing Producers followed. And every month new business added to the client roster. Many were in the housing industry or related fields. I was in the black and profitable from day one. Three months into my business Harold Burson asked me again to head up his Los Angeles office. He tells me I'm the only person who has twice turned him down that he still considers a friend. Throughout the years, he also has been a mentor.

The homebuilding industry was impacted by available mortgage money which caused fluctuations in new housing starts. For the Housing Producers I launched a campaign to educate the business media, Wall Street and Congress on collateralized mortgage notes to create a viable secondary mortgage market. I lobbied for legislation to allow pension fund investments in mortgage securities, especially where workers depended on the success of the housing industry. As the Council's executive director, I worked closely with senior partners at Bache & Co. and testified before Congress and organized high-level roundtable meetings and conferences.

My life-long friendship began with Ira Michael Shepard, then a young general counsel to the Senate Labor Committee. Our efforts led to pension fund investments in mortgage securities under the 1974 Employment Retirement Income Security Act, or ERISA legislation. This created a viable secondary mortgage market and stabilized new housing production. Regrettably some greedy, unscrupulous profit seekers issued junk, uninsured and uncollateralized securities on subprime mortgages that led to the 2008 Wall Street collapse of many financial institutions. This was depicted in the book and 2015 movie *The Big Short*.

During this time I worked closely with George Romney, Secretary of the U.S. Department of Housing & Urban Development, and his executive team. He wanted me to come to Washington to be one of his assistant secretaries and I declined. In 1972 an executive search firm contacted me to be an assistant secretary in the U.S. Department of Health, Education & Welfare. I had never been part of a political campaign, a major fund raiser or a major contributor, which today are prerequisites for such jobs. Unlike the patronage system of today, during this era senior level jobs were filled by executive search firms seeking the most qualified and best available talent. Again, I declined.

Sports marketing increased as an important part of the Sunkist program and led to promotions and relationships with the Los Angeles Lakers and Jerry West. With my friend Jay Bell, who had moved from Edelman to become PR director for Sunkist, we launched a sports film library program and created and produced award-winning "how to" films on swimming, basketball and football.

I originally opened my office in Century City but as the business grew and after two years I moved back to Westwood on Wilshire Boulevard, added another secretary and offices for as many as four associates. Rather than increase overhead, I worked with individuals who had their own business but needed the type of support I could provide and they assisted me with my clients.

I expanded and diversified my business when I ventured with Gabor Nagy and Jay Bell to form Mariner III, a film and television production company. We produced a number of award winning instructional and industrial films and audio visual programs.

Things were going so well I never considered merging or being acquired. Then in 1974, Rick Ingersoll of Allen, Ingersoll & Segal wanted to meet. We knew each other from events where our children attended the same elementary school. He and his partners were purely entertainment based and wanted to diversify. For all of us a merger made sense.

Chapter 4

Changing Times

Yes indeed, Bob Dylan, the times they are a changin'. Our new company was appropriately named Allan, Ingersoll, Segal & Henry. Overnight I now had offices in Beverly Hills, New York and Paris and new opportunities to combine corporate and sports clients with motion picture and television celebrities.

Within months, John Strauss of McFadden, Strauss, Eddy & Irwin, approached us to merge our firms. MSEI was diversified with both corporate and entertainment clients and the match made sense with the exception of having too many partners and too much overhead weighted at the top. While Eddy and Irwin had retired, we still were an inverse triangle that eventually led to the firm's downfall. We combined our New York offices and opened a new one in Washington, D.C. Our new name was ICPR.

With my real estate experience I was charged with finding office space for our new firm and 50-some employees. We leased the eighth floor of 9255 Sunset Boulevard at the very end of the Sunset Strip on the Beverly Hills border. Overnight we were the second largest PR firm west of Chicago and became *the* hot agency with an enviable client list. In each of our first three years we won Silver Anvils, the highest competitive award of excellence given by the Public Relations Society of America. This was during an era when PRSA awarded only a score of Silver Anvils compared to more than 100 today. We also dominated the awards presented by PRSA's Los Angeles chapter and the Los Angeles Publicity Club.

My office overlooked Beverly Hills and beyond to the Pacific Ocean. At dusk I could see lights turn on at dozens of residential tennis courts. We could walk to several outstanding restaurants for lunch including Scandia and Cock 'n Bull. Joe Patti's La Famiglia and Chasen's were among dinner favorites.

Hispanic and Sports Marketing

Before any mergers, I represented René Cardenas and Bilingual Children's Television promoting the PBS program, *Villa Alegre*. René and I first met in San Francisco and he was business manager for The Kingston Trio. He returned to the University of California-Berkeley to get his Ph.D. in cultural anthropology and launched BCTV. With the Ford Administration in its last year, he suggested my partners and I talk with Fernando Oaxaca, then deputy director of the Office of Management and Budget, and consider starting a Hispanic marketing division.

We did just that and became the first PR or advertising firm in the country to provide full services nationally for the Hispanic market. We approached existing clients and the program we created for Whirlpool Corp. quickly made them #1 in appliance sales in the San Antonio and El Paso markets. For too many other companies we were several years ahead of our time.

The next bold move was in sports marketing. I had been involved in sports for years. Bill Toomey, the 1968 Olympic decathlon gold medalist merged his Sports Directions company into ICPR to provide full marketing, PR, and event services for clients. One of his important clients was Coca-Cola and when its president, Don Keough, had a layover at Los Angeles airport, Bill and I met with him for three hours. It was like an executive MBA course.

Within a year we partnered with Patrick Nally's West-Nally, a Monegasque company based in London, to give us a significant international presence. A major shareholder was Horst Dassler, whose father was Adolph "Adi" Dassler, the founder of adidas. With his contacts, Dassler was *the* Godfather of Olympic and international sports.

Patrick represented the Association Générale des Fédérations Internationales de Sports (now known as Sport Accord) and most of the organization's major international federations. He controlled their events, sponsorships, television packaging, timing, and naming rights. He was extremely creative and innovative and the first person to sell site signage at sports events, starting with advertising boards placed around soccer pitches. The concept was expanded to indoor events with the signage strategically placed so it would be seen by the television viewers. He also created numerous world caliber events for his clients to further increase their revenues and is the father of sports marketing.

An integral part of our team was Jack Sakazaki, a California native and former football player and national collegiate judo champion at Cal-Berkeley, who headed his own sports marketing firm in Tokyo. In addition to television packaging and creating events, Jack was one of the very best when it came to licensing, merchandising and branding. Patrick and Jack created a score of new world class events for clients.

Our relationship gave us the opportunity to provide clients with even more services. Working together we did exciting things that included helping Los Angeles win the rights to host the 1984 Olympic Games. Our client, the U.S. Soccer Federation, gave me the challenge to organize in just six weeks a meeting at the United Nations of the Confederation of North, Central American and Caribbean Associations of Football (CONCACF) and to then organize and run its Under-20 championship. With teams from 19 countries competing at seven venues it was the largest soccer tournament of its kind held in this country. It served as a model for the 1994 World Cup the U.S. hosted. This was all before CONCACAF, which then did not even have a full-time staff, and FIFA, became so corrupt.

At ICPR I continued to handle a diverse range of clients and where appropriate would involve them in sports activities. We used sports to reinforce the image of Alta-Dena Dairy and its healthy products when the Los Angeles County Health Department alleged the dairy's raw-certified milk had traces of salmonella. For AMF Voit our campaign popularized the sport of racquetball.

Entertainment and show business was more than half of ICPR's revenue. We were the first to use sports marketing to promote a feature motion picture. In 1974 we used sports in our campaign for the movie *The Longest Yard*. When I learned that Producer Robert Aldrich was an all-conference tackle at the University of Virginia I scheduled a special screening of the film during the annual meeting of the Football Writers Association of America. Aldrich hosted a reception following with a question-and-answer period. The movie was favorably reviewed by sports columnists of every major paper in the country. When we represented MGM for the release of *International Velvet* it was easy to link the movie to Olympic sports writers. Some of the best promotional exposure for a movie is on pages other than those of the movie critics.

Actress Susan Clark was a client in 1975 when she was filming the TV movie *Babe* about the life of Babe Didrikson Zaharias. This is when she met her soon-to-be husband, Alex Karras, who played that role in the movie. When I learned that Susan spent hours learning how to golf and throw the javelin, hurdle, and high jump, I contacted C. Carson "Casey" Conrad, executive director of the President's Council on Physical Fitness and Sports to see if she was eligible for a Presidential Fitness Award. Casey was a good friend and I knew he was always looking for ways to promote the award. Carson presented Clark with awards for both golf and track and field during halftime of an ABC *Monday Night Football* game and sports page stories followed to build the TV audience.

Our significant involvement in the entertainment industry brought with it a number of Hollywood parties and during this era, invitations for luncheon meetings and elegant parties at the Playboy Mansion. Several memorable moments are cited in Chapter 15 including Hollywood being at its best with the 20th Century

Fox party following the screening of *At Long Last Love* and Carol Burnett's black tie garage sale.

Beating the Establishment Inside the Beltway

While the federal government says its RFP's (Requests for Proposal) are open for bid by any qualified company the grants are awarded almost only to members of the "Good Ole' Boys Club," an elite group of inside-the-beltway contractors who always seem to be the recipients.

Joe Honick of GMA International called me and said that he had an opportunity to bid on an RFP for the U.S. Department of Housing and Urban Development. He said he needed a team to brainstorm and then make the official presentation. The first member we added was Richard O'Neill, long-time editor of *House & Home* magazine and one of the most outspoken and knowledgeable professionals in the housing industry. Between Joe, Dick and I we had more than 100 years of experience in the housing industry. Dick and I knew and had worked with every Secretary of HUD and his or her senior staff.

For advice in complying with all federal RFP's Fernando Oaxaca was added to the team. At OMB he even had oversight over HUD. Our team led by Joe was up against the biggest names in federal contracting but for once the team with absolutely the most experience and best presentation was awarded the contract.

Our challenge and program for the next two years was introducing, educating, and explaining to the nation's housing industry MIUS, an acronym for Modular Integrated Utility Systems. A similar program would make much more sense today than it did 40 years ago since much of the energy co-generation was produced by burning garbage.

Unfortunately, we were unsuccessful in unseating a handful of contractors who had a solid lock in Sacramento for California contracts. The experience and past success of a most qualified team and creativity of a superior presentation failed to convince the politicians who made the awards to retain ICPR.

Just Like Humpty Dumpty

In the agency business sometimes you don't always get new the business you seek for any number of reasons, especially when there is competition for an account. Other times you lose business because of a change in management. And you can even make a mistake by turning down business you should have accepted. Because of the success we had with a cartoon character named Sport Billy we were approached by a German television and film producer to help launch a cartoon series in the U.S. We listened as he explained it was all about some 20 small blue creatures that live in mushrooms in the forest with just one female. He added that they wear white caps and white trousers with a hole for their tails and sometimes an additional accessory that identifies a personality or job and these little comic creatures love to eat sarsaparilla leaves. We weren't that excited about the success of the project and also considered it a conflict with Sport Billy. Two years later we lost the Sport Billy account while the Smurfs went on to a fantastic success.

We made other mistakes after beginning with a series of successes. With six partners there were widely diverse management styles and financial goals and incentives. Rather than electing a chairman or CEO, three of us served as the executive committee that ran the company – John Strauss, Mort Segal and me.

I was the only partner who hired at the entry level and trained and developed young talent. We were growing too quickly and my partners wanted only experienced and expensive senior people who were ready day one. We made the mistake of giving one woman privileges and a title as a partner without any financial responsibility or accountability. She did not share our basic principles and created several disruptive incidents before leaving to start her own company and taking with her a number of clients. When Rupert Allen, one of our founding partners, left it further impacted the firm's image.

While I wanted to recruit at the entry level and build from within my partners did not have the patience or want to take the time to train and mentor young talent or promote from within. We had two young secretaries who wanted greater responsibility but were not given the opportunity. Marsha Robertson and Frankie Lee Slater left and had very successful careers that included being vice presidents of public relations at MGM and Goldwyn Studios, respectively. Dick Taylor, a vice president-account supervisor, left with clients to become president of Rogers & Cowen and then Hill & Knowlton. He later become a very successful entertainment entrepreneur in Palm Springs. Vice presidents Cliff Dektar and Murray Weissman followed. Cliff was the very best media planter I ever worked with and was one of the most versatile in the business serving clients ranging from individual celebrities and television programs to corporate giants 3M and Whirlpool. Murray launched his own firm that later became Weissman/Markovitz and was an industry icon who became the "go to" person for successful campaigns for Oscar, Emmy, Golden Globe and other entertainment awards.

By 1980 I was unhappy with what ICPR had become and saw no positive future. I left with several clients and a year later teamed with Harry Carlson and Don Smith of Carlson, Rockey in New York to land Southland Corporation for its 7/Eleven Olympic marketing efforts.

Don Smith and I partnered for more than five years with Southland as our principal client until 1986 when a new management team turned away from Olympic sports to auto racing. He was one of the best writers and grammarians I've worked with. A few of his pet peeves included journalists who use the post office abbreviations for states rather than those in the Associated Press Stylebook; when the media refer to a "new" world record rather than just a record or world record; and calling an event the First Annual when it is not an annual event until its second year.

After I left ICPR, Frank McFadden retired and John Strauss left to form his own company leaving only Rick Ingersoll and Mort Segal. By 1982 the company was bankrupt. The firm truly became an inverse pyramid with no ground support and like Humpty Dumpty, fell and cracked wide open.

Changing Times | 33

New York, New York

I had commitments to clients that required me to be in Los Angeles through the Olympic Games so when my close friend Fred Schaus was named athletic director at West Virginia University in 1982 and asked me to be his deputy with a guarantee I would succeed him when he retired I had to decline. We became friends in 1954 at WVU when he was basketball coach and I was the sports information director. Our friendship continued in Los Angeles when he was coach and then general manager of the Lakers professional basketball team. His offer was very tempting to return to Morgantown and college sports but he could not wait for two years for me.

Following the most successful Olympics ever, in 1985 I moved to New York City because of a long-distance romance that had been off-and-on for several years with Karen Dahle, the first woman staff announcer for NBC. Our relationship was great when I was in New York monthly and when she was in Los Angeles quarterly for SAG and AFTRA board meetings. Unfortunately, it was over after three weeks under one roof. We still are friends.

I reconnected with Harold Burson and, in addition to serving my own clients, counseled Burson-Marsteller on sports marketing. Bob Helmick, a prominent Des Moines attorney, became president of the U.S. Olympic Committee and asked my help on a number of issues. He named me assistant to the president and appointed me to several important committees, all as a volunteer. I served on the Long Range Strategic Planning Task Force with David Jay Flood, a Santa Monica architect and friend. I worked with Jay for four years when he chaired the Aquatics Committee for the Los Angeles Olympic Committee and we designed the management protocol for all of the venues. For the USOC we authored the report of our task force, *A Look at the USOC in 2000.*

I spent time in Perth, Australia for a Burson-Marsteller client, Ray O'Connor, a former Premier of Western Australia who spent more than 25 years in Parliament. He headed the America's Cup Festival of Sports, a score of events prior to the 1987 America's Cup yacht race in Freemantle that I packaged for sponsorship and television.

Another project for Burson-Marsteller and its sister advertising agency, Young & Rubicam, was doing an analysis of the AT&T Pebble Beach National Pro-Am Golf Tournament. Originally known as the Bing Crosby Clambake, it continued after his death in 1977. AT&T became the title sponsor in 1986 and wanted to know the current perceptions of the tournament's image, whether or not there should be changes in the tournament, the invited celebrities and amateurs, and a new public relations program.

I worked closely with a member of the Monterey Peninsula Golf Foundation and my first interviews were with him, fellow members of the board, and the Pebble Beach Company. I had a 90-minute breakfast meeting in Carmel with a most hospitable Clint Eastwood. I quickly learned that almost anyone I wanted to talk with regarding the tournament made time to accommodate me.

A week later I flew to Vail for the final Pro-Am on the PGA tour. My Monterey contact invited me to join him for cocktails and we went next door where I talked with President Gerald Ford. While in the Ford house I met his wife Betty, Dolores (Mrs. Bob) Hope and Alex Spanos, real estate developer and owner of the San Diego Chargers. One of the first celebrities I met in Vail was Wayne Rogers, a former client, who connected me with his friends. Before the tournament was over I interviewed Jack Nicklaus over lunch. When I had lunch with Dolores Hope and Betty Ford they helped me with others including Andy Williams, James Garner, PGA Commissioner Dean Beaman and pro golfers Mark O'Meara, Jim Thorpe and George Burns.

Back in New York I met with Bryant Gumbel, then host of the *Today Show*, and Peter Ueberroth, now baseball commissioner, and had telephone interviews with Jack Lemmon, George C. Scott, and businessmen Stanley Rumbaugh, Rick Katzenbach, and Timothy Street. Even though CBS had the television rights, I got input from NBC's Don Ohlmeyer, whom I considered one of golf's best television producers. When the account supervisor at Burson-Marsteller asked me for a preliminary report of people with whom I had talked he didn't believe me until I showed him my notes.

Changing Times | 35

After only a few months of living in Manhattan I realized I preferred visiting the Big Apple much more than living in the city. It required a major adjustment from my lifestyle in Los Angeles and especially the way I shopped for groceries.

Before the year was out, I was moving again – this time to Washington, D.C.

Chapter 5

Inside The Beltway

In 1974 Congress authorized the National Institute of Building Sciences to be an authoritative organization to interface between government and the private sector and work with everyone in the building process to improve the regulatory environment and facilitate the introduction of new products and technology.

Gene C. Brewer, the retired president of U.S. Plywood Corp., was named NIBS' first president. He wanted to continue in that position forever but the board of directors in 1985 voted to bring in a new leader. I was fortunate to be the unanimous choice of the search committee. I made arrangements to wind down my business, have others take over my clients and relocate to Washington, D.C. by mid-October.

I was scheduled to move when the search committee told me that Brewer wanted to stay until the end of the year so I would not start until December. A week after I arrived at my new offices I was told that unbeknown to the search committee, the old board had given Brewer a one-year contract and office to continue as president-emeritus. Herman J. Smith, a prominent Fort Worth homebuilder, past president of the National Association of Home Builders, and my chairman, apologized when he told me the news. Had I been given all of this information in advance I would not have accepted the job. It was not the way to start.

Of the Institute's 21 directors, six are appointed by the president of the United States and 15 are elected from the building community. In 1984 Congress created a trust fund for five years to provide NIBS with up to $500,000 annually based on matching dollar contributions. Fund raising was an additional responsibility as well as meeting regularly with and testifying before Congressional committees and meeting quarterly with the vice president of the U.S. or his counsel.

The search committee told me that NIBS had become "old and tired" and "lacked luster and image." This was confirmed by building publication editors and industry leaders. But old guard bureaucrats were happy with a status quo, resisted any change and dominated NIBS and its various councils and committees. The search committee gave me a mandate to reactivate the organization with projects of significant public interest. In the first several months I launched four major projects:

- A study to use vacant and foreclosed buildings to house homeless and low-income families.
- Forums to discuss the regulatory aspects of factory-built housing.
- A report on foreign influences and impact on the U.S. construction industry.
- Establish new national land use guidelines and standards, the first revisions since 1926.

I reached out to some of our country's most prominent and knowledgeable professionals in architecture, design, finance, homebuilding and marketing and asked them to serve on project committees. This surge of activity combined with so many new faces was too much for some staff and many bureaucrat volunteers who feared loss of control. Brewer had his own office at NIBS that created dissention and a division of loyalty with some staff.

Our other projects involved hazards of asbestos, radon and lead-based paint; modular and factory-built housing; and indoor air quality. The Building Seismic Safety Council, established by NIBS in 1979, produced important publications and recommended state of the art seismic design.

The more successful we became the more the resentment swelled from the old guard and some staff. I later learned there was an underground movement to force me out. During all of this turmoil my mother passed away and 30 days later my stepfather Bill died. I was so fortunate to live in Washington – less than a four-hour drive away from Norfolk – and was able to be with them almost every other weekend.

Herman Smith, my chairman, did his best to support me as did several other directors. I found his successor, MacDonald Becket, head of a Santa Monica, California architectural firm, pompous and arrogant who only made matters worse for me.

After I was forced out, I received substantial praise from the media and members of Congress including Rep. Henry B. González (D-Texas), Rep. S. William "Bill" Green (R-New York), and Sen. William Proxmire (D-Wisconsin). One of González' senior staff members said that for the first time NIBS was doing what Congress intended it to do. She also recommended Congress halt future funding to NIBS.

Politics

After my experience at NIBS I wasn't sure what I wanted to do. A friend suggested I join the presidential campaign of Vice President George H. W. Bush, which I did. When the people heading the Bush for President Campaign saw my experience in sports and entertainment they asked me to organize a celebrity coalition division.

It became the most successful use ever of athletes and entertainers in a presidential election campaign. We worked closely with the advance teams and other coalition groups to schedule high-profile individuals to appear or perform at important events with Vice President Bush, Mrs. Bush, Dan Quayle and others.

The celebrities drew crowds, created public and media awareness and took the campaign message to non-political sections of newspapers and the media, further expanding exploitation opportunities.

Following the Republican National Convention in New Orleans we scheduled the Vice President for the successful Labor Day sendoff from Disneyland of the U.S. Olympic Team. Following the 1988 Games in Seoul, Korea, we invited Olympians to join Bush at events where he was speaking. Many did so and in their uniforms.

We had a coalition of 105 Olympians of the 335 athletes who supported Bush. Others included 42 professional golfers, 103 former or current professional football players, 51 former or current major league baseball players, and 34 others including professional team owners and stars in other sports. The entertainment side of 174 included 77 actors and actresses, 35 Nashville Country and Western entertainers, 13 comedians, and 41 singers and musicians.

The supporters included people of all ethnicities, sexes and ages. One of my biggest problems was getting past the liberal Democrat agents and Hollywood publicity flacks to contact the celebrity directly. I even had several of them call me and tell me to stop using their client's name as a Bush supporter even though I had permission from their client. Another problem I faced was keeping some of the campaign's advance people in line to not hound the celebrities for autographs or pictures.

Beginning September 26 and for the ensuing six weeks until Election Day our division scheduled entertainers and athletes to appear at more than 90 major events. The event calendar I created helped avoid a potential disaster the night before the election.

I'm frequently asked how often Arnold Schwarzenegger was involved. It was only twice but two very important days. The first was a September fundraiser in Los Angeles when a reporter asked him how it was living in a Kennedy family to be supporting a Republican and he replied, "I've gotten used to sleeping in the garage." The next was the Thursday before Election Day in Dayton, Ohio when he said, "I've played the role of The Terminator many times but the real terminator is Michael Dukakis." That quote was played and replayed every day on radio and TV across the U.S.

including Election Day.

Without looking at the calendar or consulting my division, someone scheduled a campaign rally at the Houston Galleria. This was cancelled when I told the scheduler that a few minutes away in the Astrodome the Houston Oilers would be hosting the Dallas Cowboys and the game was scheduled for *Monday Night Football* on ABC-TV.

I outlined detailed recommendations of how to better organize and use a celebrity division for President Bush's 1992 re-election campaign. It was completely disregarded which I'm sure pleased President William J. Clinton.

The Transition

The campaign days were long. My phone at home would be ringing the minute I walked in the door and conversations and requests from California would continue most of the evening. I helped organize our election night celebration party at the Century Plaza Hotel in Los Angeles. All of our celebrities were on hand. After that event I crashed and it took me until the Christmas holidays before I caught up on my rest.

Until the inauguration, I provided help to those planning the inaugural ball and television show and authored two white papers on physical fitness and health for the policy team. I had hoped to contribute my quarter-century of knowledge and experience in housing but there was no housing policy team.

Next came an interview with the White House Personnel Office. This was a new group of individuals and not those I worked with regarding appointments to NIBS. My preferred assignment was at the Department of Housing and Urban Development. I had worked with every HUD Secretary starting with Robert C. Weaver, who was the first African-American named to a cabinet position in 1966 when HUD was created. One look at my résumé and my contact told me he was going to recommend to Secretary Jack Kemp that I be named to any of three assistant secretary positions.

While I waited, and waited, and waited for my meeting with

Kemp, I had support from three of our mutual friends – Hall of Fame Football Coach George Allen; John Argue, who headed the committee that brought the 1984 Olympic Games to Los Angeles and Kemp's college roommate; and Bowie Kuhn, former commissioner of Major League Baseball. All wrote him strong recommendation letters and placed phone calls to him. They received the same form letter response and it was obvious Kemp never was told of their calls. His handlers built their Chinese wall.

Finally, my White House contact told me my meeting was set at HUD. When I arrived it was not with Kemp but a brash young man who most recently had been with a right-wing think tank. After he told me every assistant secretary position the White House had recommended me for had been filled, he asked, "Mr. Henry, would you be willing to serve as a deputy." I responded, "Of course. While I've been in the business for more than 30 years I always look forward to learning from someone who has far more knowledge and experience." The "interview" was over in 12 minutes. I subsequently learned that not one person he named had any experience with HUD or in housing or had even volunteered in the Bush campaign. That became a lesson in politics for me.

Because of the procrastination at HUD and the end run Kemp's handlers did around the White House personnel office almost every important presidential appointment had been filled. I was sent temporarily to the Department of Agriculture to help at Farmer's Home Administration. With my housing experience I contributed to a position paper for the Economic Policy Council on Rural Development prepared for the President's Interagency Rural Development Strategy Task Force.

Some weeks later I was sent to the Agency for International Development at the State Department. Because of my experience I expected to be the assistant administrator for Latin American and Caribbean Affairs but was told my job was to be assistant administrator for public affairs. Sen. Jesse Helms (R-North Carolina) chaired the Senate Foreign Relations Committee and not only did not like USAID but previous candidates for public affairs were never confirmed because he thought the position was a waste of money. During the Senate confirmation process I decided to return to the real world and withdrew my appointment.

I reconnected with friends in executive search. I resumed doing projects for Burson-Marsteller and spent time in Melbourne, Australia, helping the city with its bid for the 1996 Olympic Games. The Aussies had an excellent plan but did not understand the politics involved. Atlanta won the bid.

Making a Difference

My friend Jan Ellis, who was my deputy during the Bush presidential campaign, called and asked me to meet with her and colleagues at the Department of Labor. That led to my working for Cari Dominguez and her team that included Jan and also Jude Sotherlund, who soon went on maternity leave, to implement the *Glass Ceiling Initiative*. Cari later became an assistant secretary at Labor and under Bush #43 chaired the Equal Employment Opportunity Commission.

This job did not require Senate confirmation. I started immediately undertaking projects that helped women and minorities seeking jobs in the building and construction trades.Labor was no different than so many other federal departments and agencies and had its share of people in positions who were politically connected but not professionally qualified. Jude and I prepared a report on the *Glass Ceiling Initiative* that had to be approved by the department's director of public affairs. He changed "Foreword" to "Forward" and insisted he was right and we were wrong. We could not convince him otherwise and the report was published with his Forward!

It is difficult for people working in federal service to really make a difference and leave a footprint but the *Glass Ceiling* project was one of the most significant efforts made by the federal government to create employment and promotion opportunities in corporate America for women and minorities. I was proud to be part of that team.

More than a quarter of a century later gender disparity

continues and regardless of what political party is in power no one is taking action to resolve the problems of equal opportunities and equal pay for women.

With much of the team's work accomplished and having no desire to work again in another presidential election campaign, I looked for my next opportunity outside of government. It came from Texas A&M University deep in the heart of Texas.

Chapter 6

Deep In The Heart Of Texas

Texas A&M is located in College Station, Texas, 100 miles from Houston, 107 from Austin, 170 from San Antonio and 181 from Dallas. Aggieland is indeed in the heart of Texas. The airport gateways are Dallas and Houston and there are frequent commuter flights to and from both cities.

In 1991 I was hired on a Wednesday by Dr. William H. "Bill" Mobley, president, and Dr. E. Dean Gage, provost, to be executive director of university relations and one of five people on his executive cabinet. The next day Mobley asked me to start work on Sunday to help resolve a crisis – sexual harassment charges against the university's elite Corps of Cadets.

During a break in our meeting he told me most of Monday would be spent on another crisis – one that involved the athletic department and the National Collegiate Athletic Association.

During the next five years I was challenged with every possible type of crisis and far more than I had encountered in my previous 25 years combined. Two offices that previously had seldom worked together were combined to create what was to be my new department of university relations. In addition to the two crises, I was given three priorities:

- To develop a communications campaign strategy and plan that included collateral materials and special events for a $500 million capital campaign, the largest then undertaken by any public university. We reached our goal eight months ahead of schedule and topped out with more than $700 million.
- To head off the Texas legislature's mandated 10 percent budget cut for higher education. I contacted my counterparts at the Universities of Texas, Houston and Texas Tech and for the first time these competing universities worked together on a collaborative effort. My office did the market research and created a proactive, comprehensive, mass communications and public awareness campaign to sell all Texans on the benefits of higher education. Using sports to sell the message was an integral part of the campaign as were separate efforts directed at Hispanic and African-American audiences. The mandated cut was rescinded and the result was a 6.8 percent budget increase or $560 million more for higher education.
- To create a campaign with materials and events to raise $85 million for the George H.W. Bush Presidential Library and Museum to be built on campus. This was concurrent with the university's fund raising effort.

I quickly learned about the sense of pride, loyalty and generosity of Texas A&M alumni and friends and a sense of comradery I have not seen at any other college. Aggie tradition and loyalty are of utmost importance at A&M.

- I was pressured to immediately make personnel and policy changes in my new office. I only wish I had not been rushed and had six months or longer before I had to make such important decisions. By then I would have known the employees I could trust to accomplish our objectives and would have named

Lane Stephenson, who had headed the public relations office, as my principal deputy. He was a consummate professional and as a colonel in the Marine Corps had established guidelines that held employees responsible for their work. I soon realized I had inherited a few dissidents who did did not want to be accountable. I address some of these issues in more detail in Chapter 13. These same people resented it when I began requiring time sheets, establishing project timelines and deadlines and other basics for an efficient and effective organization.

- A policy I added from my agency days was to have the individual responsible for anything being printed to confirm with signature and date the quantity, color, binding and all other specifications on the mechanical[3] or blueline[4]. The signature of a second person confirmed it had been proofread and was ready to be published. One time when an individual did not follow this policy 60,000 copies of the University Handbook had to be reprinted because big and bold on the front cover the title was misspelled "universtiy." This costly error, which impacted my office budget, would have been prevented had the individual followed office procedure.

As I was merging the two offices I integrated it in many ways and destroyed its glass ceiling. My first hire was Sherylon Carroll, a young, very bright and personable African-American woman who was born and raised in College Station, graduated from A&M, and who had worked for a local radio station. I am proud that she has since been promoted to my former job. My second hire was Marta

---

3 Before digital technology, graphic designers and commercial artists used mechanicals which had type and illustrations mounted on boards from which the printer made negatives and plates.

4 An inexpensive contact photographic proof from negatives where all colors are in blue. Also called a brownline based on its color. This is used primarily to check accuracy and position before printing plates are made.

Deep In The Heart Of Texas | 47

Diaz, a Hispanic woman I recruited from Mexico City. They were the first minorities in the office.

We then became the first university to syndicate Spanish language radio features to some 150 stations; the first to use video to communicate to alumni; the first to use video for fund raising; the first to produce a video annual report; and the first to use 100 percent recycled paper with 100 percent post-consumer waste for all stationery and publications. In addition to Lane Stephenson, I was fortunate to have Patsy Albright and Lillian Fickey Scarmado as part of my team.

I quickly learned the importance of turfs in higher education and why this is one reason higher education costs keep rising. Several colleges and departments had their own communications offices and the very best equipment and technology. But some were unwilling to share their state-of-the-art facilities and equipment. The medical school had a little-used small television studio with modern digital equipment that neither our office nor the campus public television station could afford. The med school also had a seldom-used photography studio, cameras, and darkroom superior to the one that served the campus at large. I believe this duplication problem exists on most college campuses.

In my job I worked with every part of the university. I enjoyed an excellent relationship with the athletic department and especially R. C. Slocum, the winningest football coach in Aggie history, and Tony Barone, the basketball coach. Both became good friends.

I learned if you are not an insider don't expect to receive a grant from either the National Endowment for the Humanities or the National Endowment for the Arts. For several years I worked with faculty, our campus public television station and friends in Hollywood to propose a half dozen programs. I and every member of my team of hosts, producers, directors and writers belonged to either or both the Academy of Television Arts and Sciences and Academy of Motion Picture Arts and Sciences. Most had been nominated for an Oscar or Emmy and several were recipients. When not one of our proposals received a grant, under the Freedom of Information Act I asked for the "reviews" given by the judges. When one wrote "I do not find this team capable of undertaking this project" I knew I was wasting everyone's time. Not one member of the review panel belonged to either academy or would probably even qualify.

We created and produced several television programs but gaining access to the PBS network was another problem. Unless you partnered with one of the primary gateway PBS stations you had no choice but to syndicate the programs yourself, which we did. The gateway stations I talked with wanted a 100 percent markup just to open the doors to the network. I was fortunate to have Nate Long, a former client and friend, on sabbatical for two years to lend us his expertise. He was the first Black in the Director's Guild and an Emmy nominee. We worked together at ICPR on award-winning projects when he headed Television for All Children (TVAC).

Even Lawyers Lie

Aggie crises never seemed to end. Early on I realized that I needed to rebuild our relationship with the *Dallas Morning News* so I met several times with its top three editors. During one meeting they told me problems their reporters were having with the university lawyers regarding open records requests. That prompted me to have Mobley meet with the editorial board so he could hear it himself. During the two-hour meeting the editors showed him forged and altered documents and cited cases of where A&M lawyers had misled and even lied to reporters. Before we reached the elevator to leave the building I was the A&M open records officer. Other notable crises included:

- Indictments and convictions by the Brazos County Grand Jury of 12 senior employees, including two vice presidents, the executive assistant to the president, the athletic director and heads of several faculty departments for altering documents to disguise the purchase of alcohol. My efforts were impeded when an individual in the president's office lied to me regarding her involvement. It was ironic that it was legal to use the funds to purchase alcohol for receptions and events but illegal to falsify the receipts.

- Environmental racism charges and a lawsuit when the pig farm was relocated from the site of the future Bush Library and impacted more than 100 low-income Black families, most of whom were hourly university employees.

- Several charges of sexual harassment and date rape against members of the Corps of Cadets and its Fightin' Texas Aggie Band.

- Allegations against a distinguished professor of chemistry for scientific misconduct and alchemy.

- The chairman of the board of regents was indicted and found guilty for using his position for personal gain and profit.

- The chairman of the board of regents and a vice president were indicted and found guilty for taking expense paid trips, with wives, to New York while renegotiating a bookstore contract with Barnes & Noble.

- A racist political cartoon in the student newspaper against a Black legislator. Governor Ann Richards was outraged. When the editors and cartoonist refused to apologize and the faculty advisor considered it "First Amendment Free Speech" I issued a news release publicly apologizing for A&M. This was further compounded when a fraternity had a racist themed party.

- Theft of the university's new puppy collie mascot Reveille six days before the 1994 Cotton Bowl football game.

- Settlement out of court for $35 million when the administration showed favoritism in negotiating a utility cogeneration plant contract that subsequently was canceled.

In 1994 Mobley was named chair of the A&M System and Dean Gage served as interim president. Gage withdrew his candidacy the week before the search committee was to announce the new president. The committee chose Ray Bowen, an Aggie who was president of Oklahoma State. I attended receptions for the candidates and when I met him I did not have good feelings about working with him as I had with Mobley and Gage.

The first two things Bowen brought to his office were from his student days in the Corps: his senior boots and saber. That night I updated my résumé and began a job search. Two colleagues who were senior members of the president's cabinet were soon gone. Six months later Bowen "retired" me.

The first year I lived in Texas I was given a plaque that read "Life's too short not to live it as a Texan." I since have crossed out "not" with a thin piece of red tape.

From Aggieland to the City of Brotherly Love

As I began seeking a new job friends in executive search reminded me I was now 63 years old, that I had been away from the for-profit sector a long time and I had done such a good job as part of the *Glass Ceiling* team at the Department of Labor that many of their clients wanted only women and minorities in pools of candidates. I was fortunate that I could tailor my résumé for jobs in sports marketing, public relations, association management, entertainment, housing and construction, and higher education.

A friend at Korn Ferry warned me to prepare for at least 18 months of job seeking. I applied for nearly 250 jobs where I met all qualifications. I was one of three-to-five finalists and interviewed for 35. Looking back at some of the places where I might have been living I am thankful I was not chosen.

My first offer came from the U.S. Environmental Protection Agency and in September 1996 I was on my way to Philadelphia to be director of communications and government relations for the Mid-Atlantic States region. Customer service and FOIA (Freedom of Information Act) fell under my responsibility. Unlike my time in Washington where I was a presidential appointee this position was career federal service.

During my second week as I was getting settled, Michael McCabe, the regional administrator to whom I reported, told me that I was "lead region" and within the next month needed to organize a meeting of my counterparts from all 10 EPA regions. Being lead region meant interfacing with headquarters in Washington and coordinating various activities throughout the regions.

I soon learned that I had the best team in EPA of professionals in media-public relations, government relations and customer service. McCabe also assigned me a deputy who had been the director of another office in our region. He was extremely helpful because he knew everyone and took over the responsibility for the budget, finances, and bureaucratic paperwork.

It was a delight working for McCabe. One of my first projects was to publish a regional annual report to let those we serve know our priorities and what we were doing. This was sent to the leaders of business, industry, government and members of Congress and their staffs that we served in the District of Columbia, Delaware, Maryland, Pennsylvania, Virginia and West Virginia. This was the first such report published by our region and possibly any other EPA region. My fourth and final report was ready to go to press when I retired but the regional administrator appointed by George W. Bush killed it.

In 2000 to celebrate the 30th anniversary of EPA, McCabe wanted all 10 regions to publish annual reports with a similar theme, graphics, design and information. I held several meetings with my nine counterparts to agree on the theme and editorial material that would be localized. When McCabe moved to Washington as deputy to administrator Carol Browner his successor, Bradley M. Campbell, kept everything on track.

Getting EPA to Practice What It Peaches

Another early project was to get EPA to practice what it preaches. With McCabe's support our region adopted as policy that all paper used for stationery or any printing would be 100 percent recycled with 100 percent post-consumer waste as I had done at Texas A&M. Our head of purchasing said it saved the region money because it was cheaper than the paper he was buying. For printed publications we added the use of vegetable based rather than petroleum based inks.

We sought first to make this an EPA agency-wide initiative and then have it become policy for all federal departments and agencies but immediately hit a bureaucratic road block at headquarters. I was lucky to have the help of William "Bill" Wisniewski, deputy regional administrator, who alleviated the resistance. In one meeting he reminded the bureaucrat who was our major obstacle that in due time it would be EPA policy. When McCabe succeeded Browner within days it became agency policy but was never followed in the Bush #43 administration.

Another policy I established involved the distribution of news releases that announced enforcement action. When I learned that these stories were distributed to the media after 5:00 p.m. on Fridays or the day before a holiday I said this was professionally unethical. I believed even if a company was being cited for environmental misconduct we had a responsibility to allow it to respond to the media. My new policy was that all such news releases would be distributed no later than 12:00 noon and the public relations people at the company being cited would be given a one-hour advance notice.

This did not sit well at all with Department of Justice lawyers. One demanded a return to the old "hit-and-run" blindside sham. He was obstinate when I said that the only way I would agree is if the release included his home telephone and cell phone numbers so the media could contact him. Being his bureaucratic best he refused.

Since I was frequently in Washington as part of my lead region duties I made a point of getting acquainted with the head of public affairs at Justice and his senior staff. It resulted in an excellent working relationship. Then one day Patrick Boyle, a former managing editor of the *Pittsburgh Press* who headed media relations, pointed out 17 grammatical errors in a news release a DoJ lawyer wanted distributed. One error I will never forget was the lawyer's use of *its'*, a plural possessive of its or the contraction it's.

I called my DoJ contacts and they said the lawyer demanded that no changes could be made to any story he approved. I told Pat to release the story but to put a note to the editor at the top that it may have grammatical errors and was written by (name of lawyer) with his contact information. I gave McCabe a copy the way Pat marked it in red ink with a copy of the way we distributed it to the media. McCabe sent it to Browner who sent it to the Attorney General. My counterparts at DoJ loved what I did and said they no longer had problems correcting any errors by this or any other lawyers.

We also had a policy of being open and transparent on everything we did. A responsibility for my office was handling FOIA requests. We followed the law in timing of responses which was 10 business days. We may have been the only federal agency that obeyed the law. When a request was received it was logged in, given a number, and a return notice sent within 72 hours.

With regard to transparency, Pat Boyle called me again when I was out of town. Our enforcement division found asbestos in Valley Forge National Park the week before Memorial Day Weekend. He had the story ready to release but the head ranger in the park refused to sign off and said it had to wait until Tuesday after the holiday because it was the park's busiest and most profitable holiday of the year. After going back-and-forth Pat arranged a conference call. The ranger was adamant and said he would call the lawyers at Department of Interior. I reminded him we had an obligation to the public and once we knew of any danger we would go public. The conversation abruptly ended when I told Pat to send the news release out the minute we ended the call. It is tragic and I believe criminal that the people involved with the 2015 Flint, Michigan lead water crisis, and especially those at EPA, did not share our philosophy.

EPA also has turned its back on the carcinogenic ground rubber tires used in artificial turfs throughout the U.S.

To further build relationships with the environmental agencies in the Mid-Atlantic States I organized meetings for continued professional development. We developed an agenda and professionals and friends from the private sector gave of their time for presentations and to serve on discussion panels. My team reached out to counterparts in other federal departments and agencies but most had no interest in participating.

I loved living in Philadelphia and my condo was in the heart of Society Hill and the historic district. I walked past historic Independence Hall every day on my way to work. I loved my team and my colleagues and friends at EPA but after two harsh winters and the fact that I did not believe I could continue operating as successfully in the new Bush #43 Administration I resigned in October 2001. Following my departure, one of the first things the new regional administrator did was to break up my team into several different departments and name as my successor someone who had little professional experience. The new annual report was ready for the printers but was never published.

Chapter 7

A Taste Of Retirement

When I knew the time was coming for me to retire, I wasn't sure where I wanted to retire. I considered a number of places. In 2001, when I decided to leave EPA, my daughter Deborah was living in New York and my son Bruce and his family were in Salt Lake City. Neither city interested me. My friend John Meek kept pushing me to live in Arizona. I visited him several times in Green Valley, a community 30 miles south of Tucson. John ran the Washington office for Daniel J. Edelman when I headed the Los Angeles office. When I lived in Washington we socialized regularly and played tennis several times a week.

I bought a typical Southwestern adobe house in John's community a few months before I officially retired and moved from Philadelphia. I quickly became a part of his tennis group and played several times a week until winter came and then refused to play at 8:00 a.m. in weather colder than 45 degrees. Every month I took a two-to-three-day trip somewhere in the state to see scenic Arizona.

My college class president, Bud Jay, was a part-time resident and we met several times a month for lunch. Sometimes we would drive to Nogales, Mexico or Tubac, a nearby art colony. By 8:00 p.m. the streets were dark in my neighborhood and I tired of going to restaurants that did not have no smoking sections. I realized

Green Valley would be more appropriately named Geezer Valley.

I was keeping busy. Almost monthly I was asked to speak on crisis management and other topics at conferences and conventions. I also wrote opinion pieces for several media outlets.

Two years later Deborah was living and working in Seattle and Bruce had been transferred by Coca-Cola to Redmond across Lake Washington. I realized Green Valley was a place where people went to die so in 2003 I moved to Seattle.

Lured Out of Retirement

Residents call Seattle the Emerald City. More appropriately it should be called Oz and the mayor given the title of Wizard because of its very progressive, liberal politics. When I lived in San Francisco in the 1960s I visited Seattle often for meetings with a client, Simpson Timber Company.

Shortly after I moved to Seattle I received a call from an attorney to help turn around crisis problems for his client. Our mutual friend Jude Sotherlund, from my Labor Department days, recommended me. I flew to Washington, D.C. for a meeting with Jeffrey Prosser, chairman, president and CEO of Innovative Communication Corporation. After the interview I was walking to meet a friend for lunch and received a cell phone call that I was hired. What was supposed to be a part-time job for several months turned out to be 24/7 for three years.

ICC's headquarters were in Christiansted, St. Croix, U.S. Virgin Islands. The management office was in West Palm Beach where I was given a furnished apartment on a top floor of a building on the inland waterway with magnificent views across Palm Beach Island to the Atlantic Ocean.

My office was next to Prosser's and I was one of six people who reported to him. In the U.S. Virgin Islands he owned the local, long distance and cellular telephone companies; the Internet provider; local television station; Pulitzer-prize-winning *Virgin Islands Daily News*; cable television provider; and the island's oldest bank. ICC had one or more of these telecom and media operations in the British Virgin Islands, Sint Maarten, Saint-Martin, Guadeloupe and Martinique. The company had sales of $1 billion a year with some 1,000 employees.

In late 2003 the Central American government of Belize solicited Prosser to buy its telephone company. Belize Prime Minister Said Musa and Minister of Finance Ralph Fonseca initiated discussions with two ICC board members – Sir Shridath "Sonny" Ramphal and Sir Ronald Sanders. Both were international diplomats and Ramphal had been the longest serving Secretary General of the Commonwealth of Nations.

Musa and Fonseca saw what Prosser had done to significantly improve telephone companies in other countries and wanted him to take Belize to the next level. The government purchased Belize Telecommunications from Lord Michael Ashcroft to sell it to ICC. Ashcroft, a billionaire who owned much of Belize, was not a willing seller. The US$89 million purchase was the single largest business transaction in Belize. With an initial payment of US$52 million on April 1, 2004, ICC took control of BTL Ashcroft had a British national as chairman and Prosser said his long range goal was to have a Belizean in that position.

I soon found myself working with four different foreign governments and several departments and agencies of the U.S. government. This required extensive travel to our operations throughout the Caribbean and Central America as well as Washington, D.C. and New York City. When I traveled with Jeff it was on his custom Boeing 727. The company had two Beech Aircraft King Air planes based in St. Croix that were used for daily trips between St. Croix and St. Thomas and other nearby islands. However, it was a long commute home to Seattle every four-to-six weeks.

John Vondras, a former ICC director, was named CEO in Belize and greatly improved employee morale and customer service and increased revenues and profits. As the CEO he had led other companies through turbulent times during severe national economic crises and multiple changes of ownership including one in Indonesia that was a joint venture with USWest.

A Taste Of Retirement | 59

Within months Vondras had doubled the speed for the Internet; expanded, rehabilitated and upgraded lines for 2,300 customers adding high speed Internet and email; provided cellular service to more than 30,000 customers; announced a plan for low-income Belizeans to have phone service for the first time and for only $5 a month with no deposit or installation fees; invested $25 million to provide more than 5,000 new telephone lines giving many rural customers service for the first time; added 665 new public pay telephones with new installations in schools and strategic areas; and completed a four-way backup on the system with satellite and fiber through Mexico and the undersea cable.

At the request of Musa and Fonseca, the company further helped the Belizean government alleviate some of its debts by buying a bankrupt competitor. During all of this, however, Prime Minister Musa had not filled many of his promises. As part of the purchase agreement, Ashcroft and his Carlisle Holdings were to dispose of 100% of their stock and never be involved in any telecommunications business in Belize. This and six other major points were in a letter that Musa had yet to sign. The government did not own some minority shares that ICC could not acquire. Ashcroft hardly waited a month before he began acquiring stock from minority shareholders through companies he owned. He now wanted to regain control of a much improved company.

On February 2, 2005, the managing director of the Royal Bank of Trinidad & Tobago wrote Musa that because the government had not honored its commitments and because there had been a constant barrage of lawsuits and legal maneuvers by Ashcroft that a US$57 million balance due on February 7 would not be made. The bank said that the final financing would be provided once the government honored its commitments.

Two days later Musa announced the government had taken control of BTL and sold the company back to Ashcroft at a substantial discount. The U.S. State Department turned its back on Prosser but the U.S. District Court in Miami ordered the government to return control of Belize Telecom to ICC and included sanctions of US$50,000 a day, all of which the Belizean government defied. The Inter-American Development Bank, U.S. Overseas Private Investment Corporation and the World Bank all expressed serious concern over the illegal seizure of Prosser's assets.

When Ashcroft sent his former chairman to the office to run BTL Musa had to send armed police to guard the facilities. Workers retaliated and shut down the phone system including land lines and cellular and Internet access. Eight Belize unions representing 15,000 workers called for Musa's resignation. Labor unrest continued and the Teachers' Union and university students joined in the protest. Dean Barrow, the leader of the opposition party who would succeed Musa as Prime Minister, called for a "velvet resolution" and resignation of the Musa government and for new elections. On April 21, 2005, the protests turned violent. There was looting, vandalism, fires and bridges being blocked. Hospitals reported 27 wounded and four were gunshot victims.

Dr. Abdulai Conteh, Chief Justice of the Supreme Court of Belize, found that Musa and Fonseca had acted illegally, held them in contempt and ordered the return of all BTL assets to Prosser. Musa and his government ignored the Chief Justice's decision. Ashcroft now owned and operated a significantly improved company and made a sizeable profit on the price of shares he sold and what he paid when he repurchased them.

The expropriation and illegal seizure of Innovative's assets in Belize triggered a financial domino effect that led to ICC's bankruptcy. It was time to return to Seattle.

Chapter 8

You Can Fight Back And Win

I've always believed that if you are wrongfully attacked or taken advantage of to fight back. My philosophy has always been to be aggressive and proactive rather than passive and reactive. Take action if your image or reputation or that of a client has been damaged because of incorrect or defamatory information made public. In only a matters of seconds the reputation of an individual or company can be destroyed worldwide on the Internet.

Correct wrong information immediately. When misinformation is published and republished, broadcast and re-broadcast, fiction eventually becomes fact. The longer the delay in responding the greater chance the error will be republished on websites, blogs and other media.

If a publication or media organization won't correct or retract incorrect, defamatory or malicious information then the only alternative may be to retain an attorney and possibly pursue litigation.

Fighting County and State Bureaucrats

In the 1970s, Alta Dena Dairy was the country's largest producer of certified raw milk. The family-owned and operated California dairy was always being attacked by bureaucrats who wanted all milk products to be pasteurized. Several times a milk recall was ordered for suspicion of salmonella. Nothing the family did except for pasteurization could please the Los Angeles County Health Department.

We first convinced our client to not sue the *Los Angeles Times* and recommended the dairy attack the county and state bureaucrats and mount an aggressive, proactive marketing communications campaign. For years the dairy had an excellent relationship with health food stores throughout California and in other states where many of its products were sold. As part of our marketing campaign, we promoted good health through promotions and association of the dairy with the Los Angeles Lakers basketball team and the Los Angeles Kings ice hockey team.

We established an open book policy to build trust with the media. One afternoon a television reporter called who wanted to interview the managing partner. When I asked "when" she said "now." The reporter and film crew were at the front gates of the dairy. I called Harold J. J. Stueve and he immediately went to greet them and told them they could go anywhere they wanted with cameras.

The dairy sent milk samples daily to the county health department. It then began sending duplicate samples to two independent testing laboratories including one used by the state. The next time the county ordered a recall because of salmonella there was no trace of it in raw milk samples by either of the two independent labs. This was strong ammunition to suggest the health department had contaminated its sample, had erred in its findings, or had a bias against Alta-Dena.

The health department had a hit-and-run-and-hide news release distribution policy announcing recall notices at 5:00 p.m. on Fridays or before holidays. They gave the media advance notice so television could block out time for a story on its local news. A critical turning point with the media came when broadcast journalists began giving us a heads up about such releases. We had Harold Steuve ready for the dairy's response.

Alta-Dena was vindicated when the chair of the California

Legislature's Agriculture Committee publicly apologized to the Stueve family for the way the dairy had been "maligned" by "well-meaning but overzealous bureaucrats who had acted beyond their responsibility." The chair also asked the Los Angeles County Health Department to apologize but it did not. Much of the bureaucratic harassment ended.

Fighting Federal Bureaucrats

In 1971, Dr. Davis Y. Paschall, president of The College of William & Mary, asked my help to resolve a problem with the Department of Health, Education & Welfare, before it was split into three federal departments. A lawyer in HEW's Civil Rights Office issued an order against the college for discrimination against minorities. This meant a curtailment of all federal funding. W&M lobbyists and the Virginia Congressional Delegation were unsuccessful in getting the order lifted.

Several months earlier an executive search firm contacted me to be an assistant secretary at HEW. I spent a day meeting with Secretary Elliot Richardson's senior staff. In that era executive search firms were retained to find the best possible candidate for most senior level government positions. That policy has long been replaced by politics. My new business was less than a year old and prospering. I felt it was not in my best interest to relocate to Washington.

Armed with statistics of everything W&M was doing to recruit minorities for faculty and staff positions, I called the chief of staff who abruptly cut me short and refused to discuss it. I knew Robert H. Finch, the former HEW Secretary who had moved to White House as counselor to President Nixon. When I contacted him he said unfortunately he could no longer help.

I wrote the chief of staff and posed the question wasn't it hypocritical for Secretary Richardson to be attacking W&M when not only was every assistant secretary and senior appointee in his department a white male, but also an Ivy-league colleague. This brought back my memories of Madison Avenue's "Ivy Only" policy.

No one at HEW would discuss the situation or listen to any rationale so I drafted a news release for national distribution citing Richardson for discrimination. I let my contacts know my plans. The first call I received was from the head hunter who told me to "back off" and that I was "burning bridges and good contacts." I called their bluff, sent them copies of my proposed new release, and gave them a deadline. Within a week Dr. Paschall called and said the sanction had been lifted and thanked me for my efforts. Had it not succeeded, I would have distributed the news release.

Vote Them Out to Get Your Way

For years landslides have wreaked havoc for areas of the Palos Verdes Peninsula just south of Los Angeles. Expensive homes and even parts of golf courses have ended up in the Pacific Ocean costing taxpayers millions of dollars when governments have conceded to the wishes of developers. In 1961 homeowners won a $10 million settlement from Los Angeles County for allowing their homes to be built on unstable terrain.

In 1965 we lived in San Anselmo, a bedroom community 20 miles north of San Francisco in Marin County, where a developer planned a high-density project of single family homes on a hillside that the city engineer considered unstable. The engineer was overruled by the city manager and city council who wanted the development.

I made a presentation to the city council urging the project be denied because of potential liability that the city could not afford. I pointed out the costs and damages of Palos Verdes. All fell on deaf ears. Finally the president of the city council looked at me and said, "If you don't like the way we are running this city then elect your own council!"

Friends at the meeting who heard my presentation said we should do something. My wife and I recommended taking the council's advice and electing our own members. We had three qualified residents willing to run for office. I worked on campaign strategy and my wife Gillian did hands-on work in the neighborhoods. When the votes were counted all three of our candidates were elected and with a majority the city manager was fired and replaced with the city engineer. The project was terminated.

Public Figures Are Especially Vulnerable

When it comes to athletes, entertainers, celebrities, elected officials, and prominent public figures all too often there is a double standard when it comes to what the media considers news. If a crisis is involved, expect a media circus.

Carol Burnett fought back when the *National Enquirer* published this on March 2, 1976: "In a Washington restaurant, a boisterous Carol Burnett had a loud argument with another diner, Henry Kissinger. Then she traipsed around the place offering everyone a bite of her dessert. But Carol really raised eyebrows when she accidentally knocked a glass of wine over one diner and starting giggling instead of apologizing. The guy wasn't amused and 'accidentally' spilled a glass of water over Carol's dress."[5]

Burnett's attorneys demanded a correction or retraction. On April 6, the newspaper published this: "An item in this column...erroneously reported that Carol Burnett had an argument with Henry Kissinger at a Washington restaurant and became boisterous, disturbing other guests. We understand these events did not occur and we are sorry for any embarrassment our report may have caused Miss Burnett."

That wasn't sufficient so on April 8 she filed suit. Testimony in the trial said that Burnett was dining with her television producer husband Joe Hamilton and three friends. She had been invited to perform at the White House. During dinner she had two or three glasses of wine but was not inebriated. She talked with a young couple at an adjoining table. When curiosity was expressed about her dessert, apparently a chocolate soufflé, she gave the couple small amounts of it on plates they had passed to her table. Diners at another table offered to exchange some of their baked Alaska for a

---

5 *California Appellate Reports*, 3rd series, 144, 1983, Appendix California Supplement, Bancroft-Whitney Co., San Francisco, pg. 991.

portion of the soufflé and all were accommodated.

When leaving, a friend introduced her to Kissinger. After a brief conversation they left. There was no "row" or argument. The conversation was not loud or boisterous. Burnett never "traipsed around the place offering everyone a bite of her dessert," nor was any wine or water spilled and no "giggling instead of apologizing."

In 1981 a jury awarded Burnett $1.6 million with $300,000 in compensatory damages and $1.3 million in punitive damages. The judge reduced the judgment to $50,000 compensatory and $750,000 punitive. An appeals court reduced the punitive damages for the *National Enquirer* to $150,000 for a total settlement of $200,000.[6]

Ask the Captain

In 1972 National Homes Corporation manufactured and sold mobile homes designed by world renowned architect Frank Lloyd Wright. All had his 1930s art deco look. Following a successful press conference in New York City we were on our way to Washington, D.C. for an afternoon press conference and meeting with the Secretary of Housing and Urban Development and his staff.

When we checked in at LaGuardia Airport a team member was ready to check our most important visuals – Wright's original drawings. I said we can't take that chance. An overly officious agent at the gate said the drawings, which were large, had to be checked. I asked my colleague to wait while I boarded the plane and explained this to the captain who at one time intended to be an architect. He walked with me back to the gate, picked up the drawings and put them in the cockpit for safe keeping during our flight.

When we arrived at Reagan National Airport our luggage was not there. Had the Wright drawings been checked we would have not had any visuals for our meetings. I provided the captain with a framed set of copies of the drawings, a personal "thank you" letter from Mrs. Wright and had sets of prints given to members of his crew.

---

6 Ibid.

Taking on *The Columbia Journalism Review*

I've always been told to never argue with someone who buys ink by the barrel. And many lawyers too often tell their clients that it's a waste of time to ask the media for a correction or apology much less file a lawsuit.

The Internet has made it critical to correct any wrong information because millions can be reached immediately throughout the world compared to when a negative article printed in a small newspaper, posted on a blog, or broadcast on a cable news programs only reached an audience of thousands.

When I researched Jeff Prosser and Innovative Communication Corporation before being hired I read articles that called him a "world-class phone-sex operator." It all began with two stories in the *Columbia Journalism Review*. The *CJR* says it is recognized throughout the world as "America's premiere media monitor – a watchdog of the press in all its forms, from newspapers and magazines to radio, television, and cable to the wire services and the Web." The magazine was founded in 1961 under the auspices of Columbia University's Graduate School of Journalism.[7]

In 1986 when he was only 27 years old, Prosser bought the Virgin Islands Telephone Company (Vitelco) from ITT for $86.5 million. He was a young Certified Public Accountant from Omaha, Nebraska, and looked on as an outsider by many in the islands. When he bought the *Virgin Island Daily News* from Gannett Company in 1997 he angered several journalists which led to the *CJR* stories. In the January/February 1998 article headlined "Gannett's Sellout in Paradise," writer Mark Hunter referred to him as "... a world-class phone-sex operator" and a captioned photograph read: "Jeffrey Prosser... makes much of his money from a phone-sex business."[8] *CJR* took another swipe at him and his companies with a defaming story in its May/June 1998 edition.[9]

---

7 "Who We Are," www.cjr.org.

8 Mark Hunter, "Gannett's Sellout in Paradise," *Columbia Journalism Review*, January/February1998.

9 Konstantin Richter, "Sellout Revisited," *Columbia Journalism Review*, May/June 1998.

Prosser's advisors and lawyers talked him out of taking libel action against *CJR* or to even ask that errors be corrected. The story and the "phone-sex" label proliferated. Less than two years later, a page one *Wall Street Journal* story had the "phone-sex" label in a headline.[10] Again, he was talked out of any recourse. While not mentioned with a byline or as a contributor, one of the *CJR* writers now was an editor with *The Wall Street Journal*.

As I was developing an aggressive public relations campaign to build a positive image of Prosser and Innovative I had to explain these accusations against him almost monthly. For years, my image of the *CJR* and Columbia's Journalism School was the epitome of ethics and integrity in journalism. I expected cooperation when I called Michael Hoyt, *CJR's* executive editor, in May 2003 to correct its two damaging articles. When he hadn't returned my call I emailed him on May 29. With no response by early July, I called Robert Stone, a good friend and a senior executive for the Dilenschneider Group. I met with him and Robert Dilenschneider and retained them for help.

On their recommendation, I retained John J. Walsh, senior counsel of the New York law firm of Carter Ledyard & Milburn LLP. Walsh has a most impressive record in libel and defamation cases and is one of the country's most prominent First Amendment attorneys. He says an injured party can ask for a correction, a retraction or an apology. He took the articles apart not only paragraph by paragraph, but word by word. His 10-page "white paper" of November 11, 2003, refuted most of the damaging accusations made by the *CJR* reporters. From the day Walsh signed off on his "white paper," I excerpted references on a regular basis with all public and media contacts.

This was very important because within hours of the announcement that ICC was acquiring Belize Telephone one caller to a talk radio show asked: "Who is this Yankee Doodle phone-sex operator who is buying our telephone company?" Responsible journalists

---

10 Michael Allen and Mitchell Pacelle, "Island Empire: A Guy From Nebraska Hits It Big in St. Croix But Triggers a Backlash," *The Wall Street Journal*, February 1, 2000, pg. 1

listened to me. I excerpted appropriate pages from Walsh's "white paper" and faxed them to Belize with his biography.

Errors, Misinformation And Accusations Proliferate With The Internet

I continued to seek a meeting with *CJR*'s Hoyt. I wrote him a three-page letter on July 21 following up on Stone's conversation with him and expressed my appreciation for his willingness to consider a new story about the *Virgin Islands Daily News* under Prosser's ownership. I sent a July 28 letter with a story about awards won by the newspaper. I expressed disappointment to Hoyt in an August 18 letter that he had not responded to my letters, phone calls and emails.

I became more aggressive, talked with Hoyt on April 5, 2004 and sent attachments of the many awards won by the newspaper under Prosser's ownership. I asked him to meet with me and Richard N. Goodwin, an ICC director, author, Oscar-winner and former advisor to President John F. Kennedy, and his wife, author and presidential historian Doris Kearns Goodwin.

Refuting The *CJR*'s Accusations

Hoyt never responded to letters of April 14 and 19, 2004. During a May 4 telephone conversation, he asked me to detail once again everything in writing for him which I did in a May 27 letter. Here is how I responded to any reference to Jeffrey Prosser as a phone-sex operator:

"Describing Mr. Prosser as "world class phone-sex operator" at best can be called a major misunderstanding of a segment of the business of virtually every domestic and international telephone carrier worldwide – so-called 'audiotext' traffic, which included 'adult' content provided to individuals using telephone service as the medium. Guyana Telephone & Telegraph (GT&T), which provided local and long distance service in and out of the former British colony, was just one small participant.

"By the time *CJR*'s January/February 1998 article was

published, not only was it clear that Mr. Prosser would no longer be associated with GT&T and its revenue sources, but any attempt by *CJR's* reporters and editors to understand the worldwide telephone industry's carriage of adult-content audiotext traffic would have reveled that Mr. Prosser was not a 'phone-sex operator' as that term, if it has any communicative value, is appropriate only to describe the adult content providers, not the carriers, whose wires or satellite transmission facilities move that content electronically from point to point.

"I hope that the relevance of all this to *CJR's* classification of Jeffrey Prosser as a "world-class phone-sex operator" is apparent. The term is both incorrect and extremely damaging. In recent years, both Mr. Prosser and Innovative Communication have spent an inordinate amount of time answering questions prompted by the retrieval of that term from *CJR's* electronic archive in diligence searches and clarifying GT&T's role as a *carrier only*.

"Internet searches by companies or governments with which Innovative seeks to do business invariably turn up these 'phone-sex' mischaracterizations. The two words convey to readers that Mr. Prosser is engaged in an unworthy, sleazy business and therefore, must be an unworthy, sleazy man."

"The same then could be said of the officers and owners of virtually every communications, media, and cable company in the U.S. and the rest of the world. Mr. Hunter's story makes no effort to explain the difference between the businesses of content carriers, such as telephone companies (like GT&T), cable companies, Internet service providers and Internet portals, and the content provided by others they are required and paid to carry. In similar fashion, cable service operators are carriers of adult programming (defined by the Supreme Court as protected speech because it is not pornography and thus must be made available to adults).

"Mr. Hunter's article suggests that Mr. Prosser's early success in business and the foundation of his wealth have been built on his participation in a disreputable business – phone sex. Yet AT&T, MCI, Verizon, Bell South, Qwest and the other long distance carriers in the U.S. and the world and all the local or regional telephone carriers in the U.S. do the same business in the same way. All the major cable operators – Cox, Comcast, Adelphia, Liberty and News Corp., and Internet service providers and portals including AOL/Time Warner, Google and Yahoo all provide their customers with access to the same type of content, and derive revenue from it as did GT&T. The same is true of the operators of Hilton, Marriott, Sheraton and most, if not all of the world's leading hotels and resorts.

"Moreover, under the applicable regulations, GT&T could not have refused to provide carriage any more than other carriers such as AT&T could. There was a long distance carrier such as AT&T or MCI on every one of these calls.

"Publicly held companies are required to break out certain categories of revenues if they exceed a certain percent of total gross revenues. This is what GT&T did in disclosing its audiotext revenue. Major U.S.-based telecoms do not breakout audiotext income because, while the total audiotext revenues most likely are considerably greater than the total revenues of GT&T, they did not represent a significant percent of overall revenues. For example the audiotext revenues of Verizon in the Dominican Republic alone were much greater than total revenues of GT&T in Guyana. The same is true for audiotext income of Cable & Wireless when it was in Hong Kong. Neither had to show specific dollar figures for audiotext income.

"We believe this should have been explained to your readers. If *CJR* labels Mr. Prosser as a "phone-sex" operator, you would have to do so with Rupert Murdoch, Michael Eisner and presidents and CEOs of scores of other companies.

"The question remains: What should be done about it?"

The Validity Of The *CJR* Sources

In my letter I also challenged the sources used by Hunter and Richter:

"We believe that both of your reporters were misled by biased and vocal enemies in the U.S. Virgin Islands community with clear motivations to injure Mr. Prosser by damaging his reputation. We strongly suspect that these adversaries were instrumental in persuading *CJR* and/or Mr. Hunter to criticize Gannett's decision to sell to Prosser – a decision which would look like even more of a "sell out" if the new owner could be portrayed as a sleazy "phone-sex operator."

"His winning bid for the...telephone company frustrated the plans of clients of a prominent V.I. law firm who may have wanted to acquire Vitelco. By 1997-98, the law firm was representing Prosser's former partner, Cornelius Prior, who had retained GT&T and its audiotext revenue in his portfolio, in fruitless claims charging securities law violations.

"Another adversary, V.I. attorney Lee Rohn, has sued Prosser or his businesses more than 20 times in the last five years, mostly to no effect. Her pedigree as a lawyer is marked by one disciplinary action after another. She is presently facing a criminal prosecution for drug trafficking after trying to board a plane with a concealed and undeclared quantity of marijuana (*Government v. Rohn*, Territorial Court Criminal No. 113/2003 St. Croix Division). She has been criticized by the Virgin Islands Attorney General and courts for violations of ethical rules.

"On May 28, 2003, *The St. Thomas Source* and *The St. Croix Source*, issued a correction of an article written by David S. North that accused an Innovative company of making payments to Kenneth Mapp while he was lieutenant governor in the Roy Schneider (former governor) administration. In its correction, *The Source* wrote: "...the article should have attributed the statement to Attorney Lee Rohn, who has taken sworn depositions from the three witnesses. However, none of the witnesses testified or told attorney Rohn that Kenneth Mapp was paid by ICC or any of its subsidiaries while employed as lieutenant governor of the Virgin Islands.

"We believe that these adversaries are the principle, and probably the exclusive, source for the unfounded tales and implications about Mr. Prosser and his companies. 'Consider the source' is an aphorism that could have originated in journalism. Whether it did or not, I suggest that the motivations of Mr. Prosser's Virgin Islands critics fall under its principle, a principle applied every day in newsrooms around the world.

"Both Messrs. Hunter and Richter would lead their readers to believe that the only reason Prosser bought *The Daily News* was to cease constant negative attacks on him.

"In no way has Mr. Prosser or anyone in management ever suggested, much less tried to influence what has been reported on the news side. Mr. Richter quoted the former editor, Mike Middlesworth as follows: 'If you buy a newspaper you're entitled to have it reflect your view.' Any views of Mr. Prosser have only been on the editorial page.

"... The expressed fear in 1998 that the independence of *The Daily News* would be co-opted by Mr. Prosser or his business interests clearly has not been realized. The paper has remained a vigorous, independent voice reporting on matters of public concern to the people of the Virgin Islands .... In fact, [it] has flourished under the ownership of Jeffrey J. Prosser."

In closing I noted that the paper has won numerous awards for reporting and public service and has become the most honored small circulation newspaper in the U.S.

Still No Response

My e-mails and letters continued in July and August and still Hoyt would not meet with me or respond. Tower Kountze, a government affairs specialist at Blackwell Sanders Peper Martin, a law firm working for Innovative, asked his contacts at Columbia to intervene. When they declined he wrote Hoyt: "Respectfully, we ask that you or your superiors from *Columbia Journalism Review* or Columbia University meet with Mr. Henry. Hoyt ignored his letter so he wrote again to express his own frustration. Included with his letter was a complete package of all letters and e-mails sent to Hoyt. The response, nearly seven weeks later, and some three years after my first contact with Hoyt, came from Howard A. Jacobson, the university's deputy general counsel, who asked that all future communications be directed to him.

Enter John Walsh

I now again involved John Walsh who wrote Jacobson on March 24, 2006. Some key points made in the letter by Walsh included:
"Thinking that the negative effects of being falsely characterized in an academic publication written for the journalism profession would be transitory and brief, Mr. Prosser did not reckon with the future capacity of the *CJR* article, fueled by the explosive growth of electronic archives and Internet search engines, to place this mistake, highly pejorative characterization continuously before researchers seeking information about him or his business operations. Because of that understandable inability to foresee this effect of the new Information Age, no demand for a retraction or correction was made and no lawsuit filed. As a result, the mischaracterization of Mr. Prosser has been kept as fresh as if it had been published last week, playing into the hands of competitors and adversaries who misuse it to their advantage, and badly misinforming the merely diligent seeking business information.
"… the remedy for a person in Mr. Prosser's position is not likely to be found in litigation.… We believe, however that there is a remedy for this situation, one long recognized in journalism, and that is the appropriateness (some might say obligation) of correcting errors made in reporting to the public, regardless of whether the error occurred days or years before. This remedy is particularly appropriate when the error can be shown to have severely damaging effects on a person or his business years after the initial publication.

"We believe that the serious consequences of uncorrected and constantly republished damaging error exemplified by Mr. Prosser's case are an emerging and emergent problem of the electronic Information Age which should engage the serious attention of those responsible for editing *CJR*, arguably journalism's most distinguished publication. In fact, we have hoped and continued to hope that Columbia University, headed by President Lee Bollinger, a well known and highly respected

First Amendment scholar and writer, could, through its School of Journalism and possibly its Law School, play a leading role in considering the societal issues Mr. Prosser's situation presents and working with us to propose a solution or solutions. In fact, I would go so far as to hope that President Bollinger, as a First Amendment scholar and legal theorist, could be induced to contribute constructive thinking to the issue of how our society should deal with this problem of persistent, damaging republication of error."

Walsh proposed a meeting between all parties involved and asked that Bollinger be made aware of all issues.

A Suggested Resolution

Jacobson replied April 10 to Walsh saying *CJR* "is willing to consider" attaching a letter to the editor up to 750 words on the *CJR* website where the two articles appear and to include a brief statement in front of the two articles referring to the letter to the editor, and that *CJR* would reserve the right to edit any such letter.

In the first sentence of his April 24 reply, Walsh expressed "extreme disappointment" since "it implicitly indicates that there will be no meeting with *CJR* senior management or university level representatives, the question your letter presents is why an academic institution devoted to the maintenance of the highest principles of journalism would decline to meet with persons who desire to present facts which will demonstrate the incorrectness, unfairness and damaging aspects of the articles, and also consider the development of an appropriate remedy to mitigate the harm that has been done already by the articles and eliminate or limit future injury.

"Mr. Henry has been working as a professional in the field of public relations for corporate, academic and governmental institutions for more than 50 years and tells me that in that span of time he has never been refused a meeting by any journalism organization to discuss facts in the context of a claim of serious error."

Walsh outlined his points regarding the suggested letter to the editor and its length and content and that if print copies of the magazine are in any libraries that the letter be inserted in the editions and their presence noted on the contents page by a sticker. He again reiterated the importance of a meeting and the involvement of Lee Bollinger.

The Rebuttal Letter

I decided that a third party should sign the proposed letter, not Prosser, nor I as head of public relations. The signer was Sir Ronald Sanders, an ICC director and an internationally respected diplomat, journalist and author.

In our first draft *CJR* took out any references that this was the first time in 50 years any media refused to meet with me, that meetings had been requested time and again over a three-year period, and even wanted to delete the "Sir" title bestowed on Sanders by Queen Elizabeth. Correspondence exchanged in July and August and it was not until September 5 that Jacobson said the final version was approved. It was several weeks later before the letter was posted on *CJR's* website. Following is the letter:

Letter to the Editor
UNFAIR ARTICLES

I began my career as a broadcast journalist with the BBC and worked as a broadcaster in several countries of the Caribbean before becoming a diplomat and then a business executive. I was president of the Caribbean Broadcasting Union and served on the first board of directors of the Caribbean News Agency, which is widely regarded as an independent and objective news organization. I have served on the executive board of UNESCO and held senior ambassadorial appointments in London and with the World Trade Organization. I am a member of the board of directors of Innovative Communication Corporation (ICC), which is owned by Jeffrey J. Prosser, a man I have known for over fifteen years.

I am surprised that, twice in six months, the *Columbia Journalism Review* published extremely damaging, incorrect, defamatory articles about Mr. Prosser and ICC. The two articles are in the January/February and May/June 1998 issues.

To label Mr. Prosser a "world class phone-sex operator" in the first article was entirely wrong. Neither Mr. Prosser nor ICC has ever operated phone-sex companies. The description, "phone sex operator," if it has any communicative value, is appropriate only to describe the adult content provider and not the carriers who transmit the content from point to point. No telephone company — not even ones that have very deep pockets and operate internationally — can dictate the content of messages sent over its system. The Guyana Telephone & Telegraph Company, of which Mr. Prosser was a shareholder and chairman, operated no differently than any other telephone company when "phone sex" material was carried over its system. AT&T, Bell South, Verizon, Sprint, Cingular — all carry telephone messages by voice and data that originate with subscribers, some of whose business is "phone sex," and just as these telephone companies and their shareholders are not phone sex operators, neither was Mr. Prosser.

When the defamatory articles were published in 1998, the Internet was in its infancy. No one had any idea that business competitors could use this medium indefinitely against Mr. Prosser and ICC. Adversaries have hired firms to repeatedly access the *CJR* articles so whenever anyone searches for information about Mr. Prosser and his company, the "phone sex" reference is always at or near the top of the list.

These articles completely overshadow the positive and constructive contribution that Mr. Prosser and ICC have made to economic and social development in several countries through the operations of state-of-the-art telecommunications services.

The articles also lead readers to believe that Mr. Prosser bought the *Virgin Islands Daily News* from Gannett to silence his critics and suggested he would ruin the newspaper. In fact, under his ownership, this newspaper has won the prestigious Silver Gavel from the American Bar Association and numerous awards and honors from organizations including the Associated Press Managing Editors, American Society of Newspaper Editors, and the Society of Professional Journalists. Mr. Prosser is scrupulous in his non-interference in the paper's editorial policy and operations.

I write a weekly commentary that is syndicated on Internet news Web sites and in newspapers across the Caribbean, including *The Daily News*. Neither Mr. Prosser nor the editor of *The Daily News* has ever attempted to direct or restrict my writings. The Prosser-owned *Daily News* keeps the people of the Virgin Islands fully informed about events in their territory, the U.S. mainland, neighboring countries, and the wider world. In doing so, very high journalistic standards of accuracy and objectivity are applied.

It is well known that Mr. Prosser and his wife are actively involved in their local communities, are generous benefactors, and created the Prosser-ICC Foundation, which gives more than $1 million a year to local organizations in the Virgin Islands. These are facts that are easily established and that *CJR*, in the interest of its own reputation, should disclose to its readers who, at any time, can read the existing articles on its Web site that damage Mr. Prosser.

Sir Ronald Michael Sanders, KCMG, London, England

This case history was published in my *Communicating In A Crisis* book in 2008. Since then any and all references to Prosser or Innovative have been erased from the *CJR* website. I have lost all respect for *CJR,* Columbia University's Journalism School and the editors and writers involved.

Be Careful Where You Fight

Chances of winning a libel or defamation lawsuit depend where you sue and where you live. The U.S. courts require the plaintiff, or party libeled, to prove that the defendant published the statement knowing it to be false, or published it with reckless disregard to the truth. In England, Canada, Australia, the British Caribbean and other countries the defendant is considered guilty until proved innocent. The defendant must prove what was said was true and not defamatory and the plaintiff has to prove very little, if anything.

In Britain a reporter or publisher can be criminally prosecuted for commenting on the conduct of public officials either negligently or with intent to defame. Criminal libel had its origins in England in 1488 and came to the U.S. in the 18th century. There are criminal libel statutes in 17 states, Puerto Rico and the U.S. Virgin Islands. In 2009 the North Carolina legislature criminalized defamatory statements made on the Internet. Colorado and Utah have had similar criminal libel cases but some lower courts have ruled them unconstitutional because of restrictions placed on free speech.

Be sure you carefully pick your fights but always remember, when falsely accused, you can fight back and win!

A Summary Checklist

- When wronged, fight back.
- Don't delay taking action. For maximum leverage, take advantage of libel and defamation laws whenever possible.
- If the media values its ethics and integrity, there should be no time limit on righting a wrong.
- Libel laws vary from state-to-state and country-to-country not only in time limitations but definition.
- The State of Washington's Supreme Court has ruled it is all right for a politician and candidate running for election to lie.[11]
- Get the most professional and experienced help possible. No price can be placed on the value of image or reputation.
- In its Stylebook, The Associated Press says libel means injury to reputation. According to the AP, there is only one complete and unconditional defense to a civil action for libel: the facts stated are not probably true, but provably true.

---

11 Rickert v. Public Disclosure Commission, Docket No. 77769-1, Supreme Court of the State of Washington, October 4, 2007; Austin Jenkins, Oregon Public Broadcasting, October 4, 2007; Eric Firkel, Paper Chase, University of Pittsburgh School of Law, October 7, 2007.

- Most media belong to professional organizations that have strong codes of ethics and almost all responsible media will correct or retract a factual error.
- Document all contact with the media – e-mails, faxes, letters and phone calls placed and received.
- Be persistent and use all sources to open lines of communication. Don't be stonewalled by media.
- High profile individuals are always potential targets for misinformation and false accusations.
- If you are individually wronged by a fraudulent sale, misrepresentation or otherwise report this to your state consumer protection agency which most likely is a part of the office of the state's attorney general.
- Post your complaint on the Internet, blogs and social media.
- File a complaint with your local Better Business Bureau.
- An independent web-based consumer news and resource center supported by advertising is www.consumeraffairs.com.

Chapter 9

Creativity On Demand

Most professions require you to think and be creative and especially so if you are in public relations. Your bosses, clients and colleagues always look to you as the go-to person for problem solving, new ideas, strategic advice, ingenuity, and to create perfect special events, materials and publications. The challenges can be numerous and often and range from solving a simple transportation problem to getting a commitment from the mayor of New York City for a ticker-tape parade. In any business you have to be prepared to respond to any and all situations and when it is important to use your contacts and network. For years I always kept a pen and notepad on a nightstand beside my bed so if I wake up in the middle of the night with an idea I could write it down and not forget it the next morning.

Transportation

Getting a taxi in New York City late Friday afternoon in bad weather is always a problem. I was in our ICPR office at the corner of Madison Avenue and 56th Street and needed to get to the Empire State Building at Fifth Avenue and 34th Street for an important 5:00 p.m. meeting. No subways were nearby and the way it was raining I would have been drenched before walking just one block. My office manager called special numbers we had for several taxi companies. All the lines were busy. Because of our numerous celebrity clients we were excellent customers of several limousine services. In past similar circumstances we could almost always find a limousine available between calls that was more than happy to help. But no luck this time.

I asked Sharon Van Vechten, our vice president and office head, how we got large packages delivered. The typical Manhattan delivery service was a rider on a bicycle. She said if something was too large for a bike they would send a station wagon. I told her to call our service and say we had a large package we needed to get immediately to the Empire State Building. I waited at the office entrance and then ran to the station wagon when it arrived. The driver asked "Where is the package," and I replied, "Me … I'm the large package!" And I was delivered to the meeting on time.

Another rainy night in Manhattan demanded more creativity. I was hosting several friends for dinner at 21. I was with one couple at the Plaza Hotel and when we came out the Fifth Avenue entrance to get a cab it was pouring rain. We were fifteen in line and there were no cabs. The 21 was only six or so blocks away but impossible to walk in the rain without getting soaked. I looked across 58th Street and saw a line of idle horse-drawn Hansom cabs. I borrowed an umbrella from the doorman, ran across the street and asked a driver if he could take us to 21. When he said "yes," I hopped in, we pulled across the street in front of the Plaza, my friends got in and we traveled in style to 21 and were there on time.

I had a more serious challenge when I arrived in Toronto for a client meeting of the Council of Housing Producers, an organization of the nation's 15 largest home builders and community developers. Taxis were on strike. There were no limousines available and not a gypsy cab in sight. I was at the airport's curbside with the CEOs of four of the companies. They looked to me to solve the problem. Within 15 minutes I found a driver with a bus and made arrangements for transportation to our hotel. By this time two more CEOs had arrived with their wives. I learned early in my career it is always important to have cash on hand for such emergencies. My backup plan was to call the hotel manager and ask his help in getting one of their limousine services.

Telling It Like It Is

Sometimes you have to be the messenger who delivers bad news and hope you don't get shot. When I was executive director of university relations at Texas A&M my office was only steps away from my president's office. Bill Mobley was the kind of boss who would just as easily walk into your office as he would ask you to meet with him in his.

One afternoon he came in, sat down and explained a problem he wanted me to fix. For years A&M was an all-male, all-white, military school. The first minorities and women were admitted in the 1970s. In the 1990s, the Corps of Cadets, while dominant on tradition, policy, culture and influence, represented only 2,500 of the nearly 45,000 students. Every other month the university would participate in a nationally televised student forum on a subject of significant importance. Usually more than 400 campus student leaders participated. An upcoming forum was on gender diversity and anti-gay signs were posted throughout the Corps area urging a boycott.

Bill asked me to convince the Corps to end the boycott and to participate. He had already made an appointment for me with the Corps leadership and its Commandant, retired Air Force Major General Thomas Darling. I was welcomed apprehensively when I arrived. For the first 30 minutes I explained the Corp's importance and significance to the university and why its leaders should be present because of its traditions and respect. I said the presence of cadets in uniform did not mean an endorsement of either the program or of gay rights and only asked that representatives attend in uniform and listen. Every argument I made was rebutted with stereotypical anti-gay, homophobic rhetoric.

Finally, I had no other recourse than to tell it like it is. I looked at the band drum major and confirmed that at almost every football game the Fightin' Texas Aggie Band plays the theme from the movie *Patton*. I asked how many in the room had seen and liked the movie. All raised their hands. I did the same with the movie *MacArthur* and got the same enthusiastic response.

They were impressed when I told them my friend, Frank McCarthy, who produced both movies, was a distinguished graduate of Virginia Military Institute and a retired Brigadier General. I added that during World War II he was secretary to the general staff and aide to General of the Army George C. Marshall, also a VMI graduate. When the war ended McCarthy became an assistant secretary of state for Jimmy Byrnes. I immediately connected positively with everyone in the room. Then, I told them that Frank was gay and for years had lived with Rupert Allen, one of my ICPR partners.

I went on to tell them that Rupert was a Lieutenant Commander in naval intelligence and on D-Day, June 6, 1944, was aboard the flagship of British Admiral Sir Bertram Ramsay, commander of all Allied naval forces. Sir Bertram, knowing that Rupert was a writer, asked him to prepare the announcement to all in the naval command about the Normandy Invasion being the largest invasion in history with an armada of more than 7,000 vessels and 1,213 warships from the U.S., Britain and other countries.

I added that as they graduate and go into the real world they will be dealing with gays, many of whom are in military service. A couple of cadets began openly crying. Others wiped tears from their eyes. The stare I got from General Darling could kill.

One friend in the room was a student assistant in the president's office – Stephen G. Ruth, an African-American and A&M student body president. He looked at me and said, "Mr. Henry, I will be there." That broke the gridlock. Then the band drum major concurred as well. Mission accomplished.

Ten minutes later when I stuck my head in Bill's office to give him a report on the meeting, he already had the news from the Commandant and asked what I did to make everyone so angry. I told him the story about Frank McCarthy and Rupert Allen. He smiled and thanked me.

Special Events And Stunts

Special events and PR stunts have been around as long as the profession and have become a tool to get media coverage about a product or service. One of the first and possibly the greatest of showmen was Phineas Taylor "P.T." Barnum who founded what became Ringling Bros. and Barnum & Bailey Circus. He used giants, bearded women, dwarf Tom Thumb, and Jumbo the Elephant to promote his museums and shows.

When French publisher Henri Desgrange launched the Tour de France in 1903 to promote his newspaper little did he know it would become the most famous bicycle race in the world. The Miss America Pageant was created in 1921 to attract business and tourists to Atlantic City. In 1929 Edward Bernays, a PR icon, had a group of young women smoke Lucky Strike cigarettes and march in a New York City parade. For his client, American Tobacco Company, he told the media the women's rights marchers would light the "Torches of Freedom." In 1949 the Pillsbury Bake-Off was intended to be a one-time event and has become an annual success.

When my ICPR colleague Murray Weissman promoted *The Stunt Man* for 20th Century Fox he created special events in major cities in the U.S. with stuntmen jumping off 10 story buildings; being hit by and crashing through windshields of cars; and being set on fire. His campaign resulted in three "Oscar" nominations for the movie. Peter O'Toole credited Murray for his "Best Actor" nomination.

One of the most outrageous stunts we did at ICPR was for the American Song Festival. We convinced Los Angeles to close 10 blocks of mid-Wilshire Boulevard so a Wells Fargo horse-drawn coach with four outriders and songwriter Paul Williams riding shotgun in a white sequined outfit could gallop uninterrupted for that distance. When the entourage left the staging area and was in sight, a hired high school band dressed in Western attire played the theme from the William Tell Overture made popular by *The Lone Ranger*. When the coach and Williams arrived at the office building, the band played a medley of his songs. With help from the outriders he opened an antique chest filled with $1 million, the prize money for The American Song Festival.

Thanks to Mark Baron, our vice president-broadcasting, the result was 100 percent coverage by every television station and network in Los Angeles. Based on the media coverage of the stunt, our client told Mark Landia, our vice president responsible for the account, they hired extra phone operators for calls they anticipated.

Getting The Vote For Los Angeles

In May 1978 I was part of the Los Angeles contingent in Athens seeking the 1984 Olympic Games. Los Angeles was the favorite to host the Games in 1976 until Moscow submitted a bid the week before the deadline splitting the vote of the International Olympic Committee. Montreal became the compromise city. Since the Olympics almost never return to the same continent for successive Games, Moscow was the 1980 host. Los Angles was the only city bidding for 1984. However, the Soviets campaigned to have our bid rejected because of the cold war with the U.S. The week we arrived in Athens we were a handful of votes short of what we needed. Two days before the IOC vote, Patrick Nally arranged a meeting for me with Horst Dassler of adidas. Dassler, a major investor in West-Nally, the sports marketing company with whom ICPR had a partnership, suggested I meet with Tom Keller.

Dassler believed Keller could swing the necessary votes but it would be a *quid pro quo* arrangement. Keller was from a prominent Swiss family in the chemical business; a member of the IOC; president of the international rowing federation; president of the General Association of International Sports Federations (now SportAccord), a West-Nally client, and represented Swiss Timing.

I went to Mayor Tom Bradley, John Argue, who headed the non-profit committee seeking the Olympics, and Anton Calleia, deputy mayor, to get permission for the meeting and also for any negotiation. Dassler said Keller would speak only to me. I met Keller in the lobby of the Athens Hilton the night before the vote.

He was with Richard Palmer, a Brit who headed the international judo federation and a GAISF vice president. Keller led us to the middle of the hotel's dance floor where the conversation began. Politicians I had dealt with would do business this way – move chairs to the middle of the room and turn up the stereo volume so nothing could be recorded.

The greeting was cordial and Keller said if Los Angeles indeed wanted the Olympics he could make it happen, but wanted something in return. He wanted a guarantee that Swiss Timing would be the official timer. During this era, only two companies competed to be the official timer of all major sports events and the Olympics – Swiss Timing and Seiko. I agreed. Keller warned that if Los Angeles reneged it would be bankrupt before the Games began because he would insist that a new rowing venue be built and would "encourage" his counterparts in the other international sports federations to also demand new or upgraded venues.

When I reported back to Bradley, Argue and Calleia the agreement I made with Keller, they were pleased and said "no problem." The next morning GAISF, with Keller presiding, unanimously recommended that the IOC approve LA's bid, which it did.

Segue nearly two years later when Peter Ueberroth had been named to head the Los Angeles organizing committee. Keller announced he was coming to Los Angeles. Peter initially resisted and said any such decision was his to make. Since he had no prior experience in international sports or understood its politics, I briefed him on Keller's importance and what reneging on the agreement would mean.

Paul Ziffren hosted a luncheon in Keller's honor at the Hillcrest Country Club that Ueberroth did not attend. Instead they met later at the Century Plaza Hotel. I had dinner with Tom and he said he was happy and that the meeting went very well. Ueberroth and Keller decided that Longines Wittnauer, a Swiss timing member who had operations in the U.S., would be the official timer.

West-Nally, through its Tokyo office headed by Jack Sakazaki counseled Seiko. Our ICPR-West-Nally partnership had done work

Creativity On Demand | 89

for Seiko. Several months later when companies were positioning to be official sponsors or suppliers to Los Angeles, Timex approached me for help to be the Games' official timer. I knew there was no chance of this happening because the commitment had been made but I could not tell Timex why. Over dinner, three senior executives offered me a very generous fee and expense structure. I told them it would be a waste of their money because 1) Timex had no experience in sports timing at any level, much less the Olympics, World Cup or World Championship events and 2) competing against Swiss Timing and Seiko would be premature. I suggested Timex start with major sports events in the U.S. and build to international levels to gain experience and a reputation. Timex still wanted to retain me and I ethically declined. In the end, Timex hired the son of New York restaurateur Toots Shor for help. It was a losing cause from the very beginning.

Keller and Ueberroth became friends. Both Keller and Dassler died at young ages. The 1984 Olympics in Los Angeles were the most successful and profitable in history.

Circumvent Obstacles

In the PR business you have to get accustomed to people not being responsive and having to overcome all types of obstacles to accomplish objectives. As part of our Olympic marketing program for the Southland Corporation-7/Eleven we planned a nationwide tour of all of the U.S. medal winners including a ticker tape parade in New York. However, the city nearly lost being part of the celebration because of an overzealous, overly-officious gate guard in the Mayor's office.

For weeks prior to the Games my partner Don Smith had been trying to get an answer from this young woman who said she was responsible for special events, including parades. She refused to give Don an answer and demanded a guarantee of how many New York City Olympians would win medals. We predicted two – both African-Americans – Mark Breland in boxing and Peter Westbrook in fencing. Both did medal.

Finally we reached the day a decision had to be made. Our preference was making it happen in Manhattan but Chicago was our backup. Don and I were convinced the woman had never discussed the parade with her boss, Mayor Ed Koch, and was using him as the excuse for no answer. We felt Koch needed to know this and that he best be told when at home on a weekend. We networked our contacts to get to the mayor.

Don called Sonny Werbelin, sports and entertainment impresario and friend of Koch. Werbelin called the mayor at home and asked him why he didn't want to have a parade to honor the U.S. medal winners. I called Bill Simon, president of the U.S. Olympic Committee, our first Energy Czar, former Secretary of the Treasury and a heavyweight on Wall Street, who also called Koch. As we expected, the mayor knew nothing of our request and thought it was an absolutely fantastic idea. He also didn't appreciate being made the "heavy" in the situation by a member of his staff.

During his Monday morning meeting Koch expressed his outrage with his appointee and told his staff that of course New York was ready to roll out the red carpet for the Olympians. The following week the young woman called me and began profanely talking down to me and threatened me to "never do that again." I told her that I didn't need to because I had a direct line to the mayor and she would never have to worry about ever returning any phone calls from Don or me.

Plant Misinformation To Get The Truth

Sometime you have to deliberately plant misinformation – sometimes called disinformation – to stop confidential or sensitive information from being leaked and to determine the source. At ICPR we had a problem of confidential information becoming a party line. As one of the three partners responsible for managing the company I suspected an individual in our accounting department was giving confidential information to a senior executive who had the partner title but without any financial responsibility.

I took it upon myself and walked into the suspect's office to discuss specific business and during our meeting planted the misinformation. I told her to keep this in the strictest confidence and also to pull some accounting numbers regarding her favorite senior executive because the managing partners were planning an audit. Within a matter of minutes, I saw the senior executive charge into a partner's office and then I heard yelling and shouting. I got my third partner and we walked into the meeting. I told them what they must have been discussing and how I planted the misinformation. The suspect had been found and was taken out of the confidential loop as well as the senior executive.

Discrediting A Source Leaking Information

When Los Angeles was awarded the 1984 Olympics in 1978, and months before Peter Ueberroth was hired, an executive board met regularly to handle all business matters. John Argue, the chair, and I were concerned that sensitive and confidential information known to less than a dozen people was being published in the *Los Angeles Times*. This created problems for us with other media and we had an idea who was leaking this information.

I always met with John following the meetings to determine what we would report to the media. After one meeting while he was briefing me, he asked our suspected leaker to wait so they could go over a couple of issues. The suspect listened as we discussed the details of a story we would release in the next several days. Of course all of the facts we discussed were completely wrong.

The next morning on page one of *The Times* was the story the leaker had given his reporter contact. At 10:00 a.m. that day I distributed a news release with the correct facts that contradicted that story. Minutes later I was talking to a very angry Ken Reich who wrote his story based on planted misinformation from the leaker. I told Ken he needed to be very careful where he got his information because it would happen again. The leaker, a prominent Los Angeles businessman, resented me because he knew of my involvement but never complained to Argue. The leaks stopped.

Keeping Lawyers Honest

As part of its Olympic marketing effort Southland Corporation planned to have a handful of Olympians on retainer. I gave my client a simple letter agreement I had used scores of times before when I retrained celebrities for clients. My proposed letter had been in the legal department for weeks and we were ready to lose a couple of Olympians critical to our efforts because of no signed agreements.

I was in Dallas for a meeting and my client asked the young lawyer from whom we were waiting for an approval to join us for a meeting. She was adamant when pressed and said "These things take time… this is a very important document… it could have serious ramifications for the company… and is certainly not something I would just immediately approve without further research." Also her time was being billed back to the marketing department's budget.

I tired of her legal rhetoric and told her I never had a problem with this letter. I then played a game with her and said "This is a *pro forma* letter agreement right out of *Kingsfield On Contracts*. Wasn't that one of your law school text books?" She responded "Yes, of course." I asked her to check the book and try to give us approval before the end of the week.

The minute she left I looked at my client and told him there was no such book and Professor Kingsfield was none other than actor John Houseman from the popular TV series *Paper Chase*. He called the head of the in-house legal department and repeated my story. Within 30 minutes my draft letter was approved and hand delivered to us. We immediately contacted the athletes involved and their agents.

Getting Help From Contacts

When I worked for Innovative Communication Corporation I was frequently in the Caribbean. We had our own pilots based in St. Croix who had close relationships with the air controllers there and in St. Thomas. One morning I was scheduled to leave on an

American Eagle flight to San Juan to connect to Miami. The agent at the counter kept posting delays and when I got specific I was told my flight was delayed in Sint Maarten and would be on its way soon. I didn't believe her so I called our chief pilot and told him my situation. He called me back in 10 minutes and said the plane was not in Sint Maarten, had never left San Juan, and no American Eagle flights would be leaving St. Thomas that day and possibly the next because of a hurricane on its way.

I went to the counter to retrieve my luggage and much to the chagrin of the airline personnel passengers standing nearby heard me tell them what I knew about my flight and that no flights would be leaving for the next two days. I couldn't believe how fast they recovered my bag. I returned to the Marriott Frenchman's Reef hotel and checked back into the same hotel room I vacated a couple of hours earlier.

I peacefully rode out the hurricane. Three days later flying from San Juan to Miami the captain pointed out the hurricane off to our left and several thousand feet lower. It was a magnificent view of the eye of the hurricane and I regret not having a camera in my hands.

Don't Expect Airlines To Tell The Truth

Another incident with American Eagle nearly became explosive in St. Croix. I was meeting my friends Terry and Janet Bate for a flight to San Juan where we both had connecting flights. When I arrived at the ticket counter there were some 30 people ahead of us. Our flight and another scheduled to depart an hour earlier were posted as delayed. I called our company pilots whose offices were next door. They checked with their tower contacts and told me both flights had been cancelled but they had a King Air ready to fly us to San Juan.

Janet was near the head of the line waiting to get information. She and all of the others waiting patiently were being told by the agents that both flights would be coming soon and apologized for the delay. Rather than fight my way through the crowd I just yelled out, "Janet, both of these flights have been cancelled. I have a company plane for us." As a station wagon arrived to take us to the company hangar the airline counter personnel were trying to prevent a riot. We made our connecting flights.

A Delta agent in Atlanta lied to me when I was waiting for a connecting flight to Charleston, West Virginia. The agent kept posting a delay time for departure. I needed to let a friend know I would be arriving late and he happened to be the editor of the *Charleston Gazette*. He told me the airport was closed and would be until the following day because a plane crashed off the end of the runway when landing. I asked the agent for my bag and to book me on a flight the following day. When he told me there were "mechanical problems" I unnerved him and everyone around him by asking him to check with his superior because no flights would be taking off or landing in Charleston because of the crash. I added, "Why lie? Why not just tell the truth?"

Fighting Fire With Fire

My client 3M made ceramic granules that were used to coat asphalt roofing. We created a campaign to seek more stringent California regulations for fire safe roofing in dangerous fire hazard areas, obviously increasing the sales of asphalt roofing. The educational PR campaign was directed at local and state politicians and regulators, insurance companies, and the general public.

I worked with the San Francisco Fire Chief to stage a demonstration during the annual conference of the International Association of Fire Chiefs in the Bay City. We built a structure in one of the department's training areas and one half was covered with asphalt roofing and the other half with wood cedar shingles. Following procedures outlined by Underwriters Laboratories firemen began placing pieces of flaming charcoal on both roofs. Soon the wood roof was ablaze while the charcoal simmered out on the asphalt roof. After half of the structure with the wood roof burned to the ground the firemen put out the fire. There was no damage to the half covered by asphalt roofing.

It was an impressive media event and received widespread media coverage with fire chiefs best telling our story in interviews. A couple of days later my client called to say we were a success. A leading wood products trade association had sent out a letter to all of its members urging what would be an illegal boycott of all 3M products. The first 3M learned of this was an apologetic call to the 3M president and its lawyers saying the memorandum was being withdrawn and corrected. I had a very happy client.

Creativity At Its Best

Throughout my career I've been involved in many brainstorming sessions to come up with the perfect idea or concept for a client, company or organization. Looking back, I believe the most creative of all were those involving sports marketing and my partners and friends Don Smith, Bill Toomey, Patrick Nally, Jack Sakazaki, and Joe Honick. Unfortunately, we were never all together at the same time or for the same project, but being in a room with any of these five individuals you could always feel the energy flowing. Don, Bill, Patrick, Jack and I all worked in sports marketing and Joe and I on other projects and especially those related to housing and business. I love reading his opinion pieces and insights into politics and world affairs.

Another long-time friend who also is one of the most creative and innovative people I know is Shelly Saltman. He has created a score of successful radio and TV sports events and programs and was the first president of Fox Sports. I regret Shelly and I never worked together but now we talk weekly on a wide range of subjects and there is an abundance of energy. I enjoy reading his columns which always bring back many old memories. When the California Wine Institute was a client he got his friend Jerry Perenchio, business-entertainment impresario, to host a wine tasting party to honor Andy Williams. It was the most star-studded of all of my Hollywood wine tastings.

My two favorite photographers who documented everything worth photographing are Tom Vano in San Francisco and Bill

Eastabrook in Los Angeles.

When it comes to graphic design and art I consider Jack Cullimore among the very best. Jack has been a friend for 50 years and designed the cover of this book and two others I have authored. He has been responsible for the award-winning creative concepts of scores of annual reports, publications, posters and other printed material I produced for my clients. When I left Edelman to start my own business he created my distinctive RAH logo and every day it reminds me of our friendship.

When I was in Philadelphia the coast-to-coast distance made it difficult to work with Jack because of necessary personal interaction. I needed to find another outstanding graphics artist and did in Judy Munroe who also became a good friend. Her Munroe Creative Partners firm has offices in Philadelphia and New York and designed three EPA annual reports as well as the cover of the first book I authored on crisis management and communications.

Chapter 10

Gate Guardians

Executive assistant, administrative assistant, secretary or whatever you call them, they guard the gates to the CEOs and senior executives today. Some make it nearly impossible to get through to their boss by not taking time to listen to callers or read letters, emails or faxes, often short stopping something their boss should read. Then they further misdirect the query to the wrong individual in the company. Even worse there is no courtesy of a response. Some guardians today barely have the qualifications to be a file clerk.

Companies where the CEOs and senior executives are easily accessible, available and responsive are the ones that generally provide the best customer service. There is a correlation reflected by their executive assistants.

In the previous chapter, I pointed out how you have to be creative to circumvent people obstacles. This is what Don Smith and I did to get to Mayor Ed Koch for the ticker tape parade for the 1984 U.S. Olympic medal winners.

Stubbornness and Stupidity = Missed Opportunities

Gate guardians who wall off their CEO create crises. Two women cost Landor Associates, a prominent design and brand-consulting firm based in San Francisco, the opportunity to bid on a major corporate identity and logo program. When I was at Texas A&M, where the George H. W. Bush Presidential Library and Museum was to be built, I was asked to recommend several design firms to be considered for the project.

When I lived in San Francisco I was well aware of the Landor firm's reputation. I attended special events on board a renovated ferry boat that served as the company's offices. But some 25 years later, when I called to get current information, a capabilities statement and client list, I was rebuffed by both the switchboard operator and an overly officious "executive assistant." I could not speak to anyone in authority. They insisted on knowing information about the project that I could not reveal. Frustrated, I gave them my name, title and affiliation and urged them to please give it to their president.

I gave the library's director complete packages on several firms I recommended. No one at Landor returned my call so I had no information on the firm's qualifications. Today most of the information I requested can be accessed on the Internet.

Know Your Boss

Too many gate guards do not listen to the caller. The late Donald Keough, former president of Coca-Cola and chair of New York investment banker Allen & Company, told this story to *Leaders* magazine: "I called one of my associates at Coca-Cola and said, 'This is Don Keough, I'd like to speak to (name of individual).' The secretary on the other end of the line said, 'Who is this?' I replied, 'Don Keough.' She asked, 'How do you spell that?' I said K-e-o-u-g-h. Then she asked 'What business are you in?' I told her 'I work for The Coca-Cola Company.' She said she would try to get her boss to call me back at a later date." Keough never said if the secretary continued to work for Coca-Cola.

There is one gate guardian whose face I would have loved to have seen when I had a perfect reply for her. I called Eli Broad, co-founder of Kaufman & Broad and Sun America companies and a major philanthropist, and said: "Hello, this is Rene Henry. Is Eli available?" She replied, "Does he know you, Mr. Henry?" I said, "Yes, for 25 years." That wasn't sufficient for her. "Who do you work for, Mr. Henry?" At the time, I was immersed in the 1988 Bush presidential campaign organizing all of the athletes and entertainers, so I just answered, "The Vice President." Her voice was so cold it would have frozen water if I had a glass in my hand, when she curtly asked, "the vice president of what?" I couldn't resist, and almost laughing, understated, "The United States of America." There was absolute silence. Within seconds Eli was on the phone, "Rene, how are you? …."

When management consultant and author Tom Peters called 13 firms to ask a basic question or file a complaint, his research turned up everything from great service to being rudely disconnected. Peters called Yoplait and wanted to know the yogurt maker's stance on bovine growth hormones. The operator refused to transfer the call to anyone. At Ben & Jerry's this question brought a swift transfer to the public relations department and an eight-minute discussion on why the ice cream maker shuns the additive.

He called IBM to request an annual report and information regarding the annual meeting. He was transferred to stockholder relations and an enthusiastic operator gave way to a voice recording so he left a message. The information he wanted arrived two weeks after the annual meeting.[12]

When Peters called General Motors to ask why it was taking automakers so long to develop electric cars, his request to speak with CEO Jack Smith was denied. He was transferred to the library, then to a non-working number, then disconnected. When he called Nordstrom and asked to speak to the CEO about a problem with the shoe department just one transfer later CEO Bruce Nordstrom was on the line. He listened patiently and promised to fix the problem.[13]

---

12 Ellen Neuborne, *USA Today*, Section B, Pg. 1, May 10, 1994.
13 Ibid.

Gate Guardians | 101

Getting Around The Gate Guards

Sometimes it's fun to give the gate guardians some of their own medicine. With creativity, ingenuity and networking, often you can find a way to get around them.

When I was director of communications and government relations for the Mid-Atlantic States region of EPA I decided to use quotes in our 1998 annual report from famous people who were either born, raised or had successful careers in our region. My staff and I created a priority list of celebrities. As I expected, the publicity flacks for some entertainment and sports stars turned us down or never responded. How could someone in the public eye not support the environment?

After being unsuccessful to reach one actor, when I learned that his father was a prominent Philadelphia architect and environmental champion, I asked him to please send his son my request. In a matter of days, I had a great quote. The quote I wanted from an Olympic champion I got by going through her father. For news anchors and personalities at CBS and NBC I asked friends at both networks to put my requests in their interoffice mail. I soon had quotes from Walter Cronkite and Katie Couric. The annual report was a success.

Sometimes you even have to circumvent a partner. ICPR partner Mort Segal and I were having lunch at the Beverly Wilshire Hotel when a woman who was a mover-and-shaker in Los Angeles asked us for help. "Carol Burnett has always supported our charity," she said. "I've left word several times for your partner Rick Ingersoll and he has not called me back."

Once back at the office Mort called Carol. She said it was one of her favorite charities and she would love to help by doing public service television commercials. Later than day Rick angrily crashed a meeting Mort and I were having. He had represented Carol for years and more often than not always turned down such requests without ever letting her know. After he had vented his anger and began to calm down, Mort reminded him that he would have said "no" and probably had no idea it was one of her favorite charities. The result ended up making two women very happy.

Blue Eyes and Red Eyes

In 1980 I was working with Resorts International Hotel in Atlantic City on behalf of Mohawk Carpet to stage a $100,000 bicycle race that would start and finish on The Boardwalk in front of the hotel. My friend Michael Marks, with whom I'd worked when he was vice president of marketing at The Forum in Los Angeles, was now senior vice president of marketing for Resorts. He urged me to come a day earlier for a meeting we had planned. It was the last night Frank Sinatra and Dean Martin would be performing at Resorts and Sammy Davis, Jr. was scheduled to open two nights later at another hotel.

Michael had an idea to have a softball game the night before the final performance with the Sinatra Blue Eyes playing the Martin Red Eyes. Staff, friends and members of the chorus line and other entertainers would participate. The game would be open to the public and those attending would be asked to donate to a local charity. Resorts would cater free refreshments.

Lee Solters, who represented some of Hollywood's biggest names, was with Sinatra all week. When Marks told him about the idea he said he would get back to him. Several days passed without Solters responding so the next time Marks saw Sinatra he asked him. Sinatra told him he loved the idea and to make it happen. Martin concurred. Solters was outraged.

Michael called and invited me to play in the game but it meant coming even earlier and I could not. I missed a fantastic experience. In fact, Tommy Lasorda, manager of the Los Angeles Dodgers, got himself thrown out of a baseball game early against the Phillies so he could get from Philadelphia to play.

Because of his position, Michael had the best table in the house for the final Sinatra-Martin show. Halfway through the show when they were making jokes about him, Sammy Davis, Jr. showed up in the back of the audience. He came on stage and the three performed well beyond the normal time for their act. It may have been the last time the three performed together and was one fantastic evening. It was an event to remember.

Chapter 11

Always Believe In Yourself

I am often asked to speak about leadership. I believe one of the most important aspects of leadership and successful management is to always believe in yourself. If you know you are right, stand by your conviction and support what you believe. It does help to be supported by facts and documentation.

I learned early in my life that you will not always get your way. After you state your case, sense when you need to back off. Do not push too hard for what you want. A good CEO or boss will respect you for your ideas and opinions even if they are not necessarily accepted.

During my career I consulted a broad range of clients. I always sought to develop a program with goals and objectives according to the client's strategic plan. Sometimes you give a client what he or she wants and sometimes you miss. Other times you are right and the client is wrong. But right or wrong, you should have an attitude that the customer is always right.

I used not to be this way. When I was young and right out of college, I compromised too often. I did not always stand up for what I believed was right. I learned the hard way, from experience.

Taking The Wrong Road

The first time I went skiing was on a small hill outside of Morgantown, West Virginia. Several members of a ski club had me join them on a Saturday. They knew I might be skiing alone the following day and pointed out which road to take at a critical fork. They said the other road was not yet cleared and there would be a good chance my car could get stuck in the snow.

A friend I went skiing with on Sunday had been active in this club for several years. I volunteered to drive. At the area when we reached the critical fork in the road, I turned left. He said, "no, you must go to the right." I explained what I was told the day before and was convinced there would be no problem. My friend was so insistent that we go right, I did just that. Within a mile we were hopelessly stuck in the snow.

We had to work out way back to the main road, hitch a ride to the nearest general store and call for a tow truck. By the time we were free, the day was gone and ruined. It was an expensive lesson to learn when I knew I was right all along.

Always be honest first with yourself and stick to what you believe is right. I am often asked to give an example. "Stay The Course" is one of my favorites and a story I often tell when speaking about leadership.

Stay The Course

When I lived in Los Angeles, I had a sailboat berthed at Marina Del Rey. It was a Cal 2-29 appropriately named "Foolish Pleasure" for more than one reason. Because of the terrific Southern California weather I could sail 12 months of the year. During the summer I raced every Wednesday night. During the rest of the year, one weekend day was for competition and the other for pleasure with friends.

One day I was sailing in Santa Monica Bay with a date and a friend and his date. I knew early on it wasn't going to be an enjoyable sail because once we were in the bay my friend's date promptly threw up in the galley sink, rather than over the side of the boat.

Late in the afternoon I saw a bank of fog rolling in from the horizon that was not uncommon in Santa Monica Bay. I had a hand held compass and took several fixes to triangulate our approximate location. When you sail, it is crucial to be prepared and always know your location. I gave the wheel to my friend and told him the course to hold heading 90 degrees (East) while I went below, reviewed the charts and determined where I could find the nearest navigational buoy. Santa Monica Bay not only has navigational buoys with bells or horns and an identification number, but it has a number of buoys and markers used for racing. I plotted all of the racing buoys on my charts. This was the days before GPS[14].

I located the nearest racing buoy and selected a course that would get us home. Soon we were totally enveloped in fog. When we reached the first buoy, we tacked onto another course heading for the next buoy. Based on my calculations the third leg would take us right into Marina Del Rey.

The charts give you specific distances so all the navigator needs to do is check his average speed, estimate any resistance from drift or the tide and hold a course for a determined time to get the boat to its intended destination.

When we reached the navigational buoy off the Santa Monica pier we had our final tack heading south paralleling the Santa Monica and Venice beaches. The fog was very thick. Halfway between the Santa Monica and Venice piers we came along side five sailboats off our port beam. They were all in a row like ducks following the leader.

Five Boats Against One

A few minutes later, the five sailboats took a course 45 degrees away from us. My friend and our dates became concerned and insisted I follow the last boat because all five skippers could not be wrong. I said that the captain or navigator of the lead boat didn't have a clue

---

14 GPS or Global Positioning System, also known as Navstar, is a global navigation satellite system that provides exact location and time information in all weather conditions. It is freely accessible to anyone with a GPS receiver.

where he was. I believed I was right and stayed the course.

Members of my racing crew nicknamed the friend on board Candyass and asked me never to have him crew with us in a race. Others referred to him as a Boychick Goniff. True to form, Candyass panicked. He upset the women who began crying and had visions of the boat sinking, everyone drowning or us on our way to Hawai'i.

I was outvoted 3-1 and finally compromised and agreed to go below and double check my calculations just in case I had made an error. All of a sudden, I was beginning to question myself. Don't ever let this happen. My calculations were correct.

After reviewing the charts, when I came out of the cabin, Candyass, who had taken the helm, had fallen off course and we were following the five boats. I nearly went ballistic, pushed him aside, took over the wheel and felt like throwing him overboard for mutiny. When I brought the boat back on course all three were now crying.

Within minutes we were alone in the fog. There was only the sound of the boat cutting through the water. I was confident I was right. The others were trying to figure how to take control of the boat from me, but now they had no one to follow or know which direction to head.

We then heard a distant foghorn which began to get louder off our port beam. Candyass yelled out "That's Marina Del Rey … that's where we're supposed to be … we should have followed the other boats." I told him to trust me that it was not Marina Del Rey, but the horn off Venice Beach pier. As the foghorn slowly became silent and we were in the stillness of the fog, the three convinced themselves we were all going to die. It wasn't long until we could hear the faint sounds from the Marina Del Rey foghorn. Each horn has a distinctive sound and signal so they can be identified. There was relief on board but I was still as angry and I was right.

We came in dead on course exactly where I wanted to be between the two breakwaters. Once I was in the main channel, I turned on auxiliary power and only then let my friend have the wheel again while I stowed the sails. Needless to say, by the time we got back to the slip I told Candyass to take the girls home and wanted nothing to do with any of the three.

An Appropriate Finish – The Reward

Later than evening I was preparing dinner and got a phone call from Gregory J. Bonann. He was the creator and producer of the successful television series, *Baywatch*. He said, "Rene, you won't believe what I saw today. I was standing on the Venice Beach and all of a sudden out of the fog comes this big sailboat – it had to be at least 40 feet. Before it knew where it was, it was in the breakers and beached. I started to run to a lifeguard station to call the Coast Guard for help, when a second, but smaller sailboat came out of the fog and also got caught in the breakers."

At this point I interrupted Greg and said, "There were five boats, weren't there?" He said "Yes, but how did you know." I told him what had happened on what was going to be a pleasure sail that afternoon and if my fellow sailors had their way "Foolish Pleasure" would have been the sixth boat stranded on the Venice Beach.

The story was big on television and page one of the local newspapers. The incident still did little to convince regulatory agencies to do anything about making boating safer. It is the one recreational sport where if you have the money to buy a boat, regardless how big or fast it may be, you don't need a license to operate it or show any degree of competency or proficiency in sailing, boating, navigation or water safety.

The morale of the story is to believe in yourself. If you are going to follow someone else, make sure that person knows what s/he is doing. In life if you avoid confrontation and relinquish leadership, you too could end up on the beach.

Chapter 12

Breakfast With The Godfather

In 1960 one of my clients was Simpson Timber Company, a major producer of building products including redwood, doors, ceiling tile, plywood and lumber. I was always looking for projects that would show how an architect, home builder or homeowner used Simpson products in an important or innovative way.

This led me to Las Vegas where I met Irwin Molasky and Merv Adelson. They gave me a tour of their Paradise Palms housing development, the area's first master planned community. The houses, which sold for $30,000 to $40,000, were a great showcase for Simpson products. I packaged the story with photos, plans, and interviews with Molasky and Adelson, and it became the cover story of *American Builder* magazine.

At the time, little did I know the success the two men would have in the years to come. Nor did I have any idea the impact of a reprint of the cover story would have as a sales and marketing piece for their development.

Molasky was the son of an Ohio businessman who had a newspaper distribution agency and managed apartment buildings. He got an early start in housing as a teenager working summers for his brother-in-law's construction business. After a year at Ohio State, he moved to Southern California and transferred to UCLA.

He worked at all types of construction jobs, started design and construction, and built a five-unit apartment building when he was only 19. His father signed for the financing.[15]

Adelson was the son of a Beverly Hills grocer and moved to Las Vegas in 1951 to start a 24-hour food store. He and Molasky became friends and founded Paradise Development Co. The two men built Las Vegas' first enclosed mall, first major hospital and medical center, first high-rise condominium, first high-rise office building and the state's first hospice. They were instrumental in the development of the University of Nevada at Las Vegas and donated 45 acres of prime property for the campus. They both gave back much to the community.[16]

On a followup trip to Las Vegas they showed me plans for a $100 million master planned community north of San Diego. In 1965 they opened Rancho La Costa Resort & Spa in Carlsbad which became a model for the club and resort business.

Success continued and in 1968 they partnered with Lee Rich to found Lorimar Productions which became an icon in the television industry. The name came from Adelson's ex-wife, Lori, and the initials of the three founders. The first major hit television production was *The Waltons* and was followed by *Dallas, Eight Is Enough, Knots Landing,* and *Falcon Crest.* Lorimar moved into feature film production with hits including *Being There, Cruising,* and *An Officer and a Gentleman.* In 1988, Warner Communications, which was merging with Time Inc., purchased Lorimar. Adelson later married Barbara Walters.[17]

The Partners With The Money

Two principal investors in Molasky and Adelson developments were Morris B. "Moe" Dalitz and Allard Roen who became part owners of the Desert Inn in 1949. Born in Boston and raised in

---

15 Wikipedia.
16 "Remembrance of Wings Past," *Vanity Fair*, Bryant Burrough, March 20313; *Las Vegas Review Journal*, February 10, 2013.
17 Wikipedia.

Michigan, Dalitz worked in the family laundry business and capitalized on using the delivery trucks for bootlegging when Prohibition began in 1919. He became head of a Jewish American organization known as the Cleveland (Ohio) Syndicate and established ties with Cleveland's Eastside Little Italy community with whom he merged to form the leading underworld organization in Cleveland. Operations extended between Cleveland, Detroit and Ann Arbor, Michigan.[18]

Dalitz was a longtime friend of Meyer Lansky of Murder, Inc., considered by many to be one of the main architects of modern organized crime. When he was 47, he attended the famed Havana Conference at Cuba's Hotel Nacional in late December 1946. According to T.J. English, author of *Havana Nocturne: How the Mob Owned Cuba and Then Lost It to the Revolution,* a select group of 22 dignitaries caucused to strategize the American mob's plan to make Cuba a Western Hemisphere vice haven. The group included Lansky, Giuseppe (Joe Bananas) Bonanno, Vito (Don Vito) Genovese, Charles (Lucky) Luciano, Frank Costello, Joe Adonis, and Tony (Big Tuna) Accardo, former bodyguard for Al (Scarface) Capone. In 1978, an FBI official said, "The individual who oversees the operations of the La Cosa Nostra families in Las Vegas is Moe Dalitz."[19]

He had close relationships with both Jimmy Hoffa, general president of the International Brotherhood of Teamsters from 1958 to 1971, and Lew Wasserman, born in Cleveland to Russian Jewish immigrants, and head of MCA and one of the most powerful men in the entertainment industry. Dalitz was often referred to as "Mr. Las Vegas" for his efforts in shaping Las Vegas into a modern city. He was noted for his philanthropy and giving to Las Vegas community organizations. He is credited with giving Frank Sinatra and other well known personalities their first big breaks in show business.[20]

Roen attended Duke University on a baseball scholarship,

---

18 *The Green Felt Jungle,* Ed Reid and Ovid Demaris, Trident Press, New York, 1963.
19 Ibid.
20 Ibid.

graduated in 1943 with a degree in business and served as a Navy lieutenant during World War II. He was the managing director and ran the Desert Inn until he and Dalitz sold it to Howard Hughes in 1967. He is noted for integrating Las Vegas and hosted U.S. diplomat and Nobel Peace Prize recipient Ralph Bunche during the height of segregation in the 1950s. When Sammy Davis, Jr. wanted to play golf on the whites-only Desert Inn golf course, Roen played with him. And when singer Pearl Bailey wanted to leave the DI's showroom for the Flamingo, he gave her the black chorus line she wanted. He conceived and developed the Tournament of Champions golf tournament at the Desert Inn before moving it to the Stardust in 1967 and La Costa in 1969. He too was known for his philanthropy.[21]

In the 1960s, Roen pleaded guilty in the United Dye and Chemical Corporation securities fraud. He and other defendants were charged with swapping almost worthless companies to United Dye in exchange for 575,000 shares of stock, four times the amount previously outstanding. The stock was promoted and sold for $10 million. Four people were sentenced to prison, including one Las Vegas gambler, Charles M. Berman of Lewiston, Idaho, who was fined $35,000 and given a six-year sentence.[22]

The Sources Of The Money

Financing for many of the developments came from the Teamsters Central States, Southeast and Southwest Pension Fund. The Teamsters loaned $1 million to increase the new Sunrise Hospital from 58 to 120 beds and took members from the local Teamsters and Culinary union each month.

The Teamsters provided the $100 million financing needed for development of Rancho La Costa. Some journalists referred to the Teamsters Central States fund as essentially as a piggy bank controlled by Jimmy Hoffa.

In April 1981 the U.S. Department of Justice sued the Teamsters

---

21 Wikipedia.
22 *The Green Felt Jungle*, op. cit.

for mismanaging its pension fund. Accusations of malfeasance included huge loans to the Dunes and Aladdin casinos in Las Vegas as well as Rancho La Costa and La Costa Land Company – all rated as firms with a "serious negative cash flow problem." During testimony in a libel suit Molasky and Adelson filed against *Penthouse* magazine, Dalitz testified that while Hoffa was a boyhood friend, he said he had no influence over any Teamster union loans. "If I shook hands with the Duke of Windsor," he said, "it didn't make me a duke."[23]

Rancho La Costa

Molasky and Adelson built La Costa's golf courses, tennis courts, clubhouses, resort hotel, spa, condominiums, business center and the infrastructure. The new community began with 3,500 acres north of San Diego. As the soon-to-be world class development became popular, another 2,000 acres were purchased. The land was sold to other developers who built homes, condominiums, townhouses, apartments and retail outlets. And the La Costa partners wanted to attract and sell land other builders to develop.

From the time that La Costa had opened I not only attended conferences, business meetings and events at the resort, but also scheduled them for clients. One client event I organized was a November 1970 meeting for the Council of Housing Producers. I also served as executive secretary of this prestigious and elite group of the country's 15 largest home builders and community developers. While at La Costa to make advance arrangements, I ran into both Molasky and Adelson who said they would like to host a reception for my clients.

The reception was at Allard Roen's house and during the evening, Molasky and Adelson introduced me to Moe Dalitz. They told him, "Rene is the person who was responsible for that great magazine cover story about our Paradise Homes development when we were just getting started." Dalitz put his arm around me, hugged me, and with a big smile said, "Thank you, Rene. Whatever

---
23 Ibid.

you want, you just ask me!"

Over my shoulder I could see several of my clients looking at me and the way Dalitz was smiling and talking to me. The presidents represented their companies at the meetings and included Eli Broad (Kaufman & Broad), Larry Weinberg (Larwin Group), Leonard Miller (Lennar), Herman Sarkowsky (Levitt), David Price (National Homes), John Koskinen (Macco-Great Southwest), Jim Klingbeil (CBS-Klingbeil), Charles Rutenberg (U.S. Home), Ray Watt (Boise Cascade), Sam Primack (Perl-Mack), Bill Berman (Dreyfus Development), Malcolm Prine (Ryan Homes) and Frank Crossen (Centex Corp.). Later several pulled me aside and said, "Rene, why don't you introduce us to your friend?" I replied, "Oh, you mean 'Uncle Moe'? I've known Irv (Molasky) and Merv (Adelson) for 10 years. They showed me their initial plans for La Costa."

The Morning After

The next morning I had an early breakfast and needed to be sure the room was properly set for the meeting. As I walked into the main dining room and was waiting to be seated, Moe Dalitz was at the very front table. He waved to me and said, "Rene, please join me." And I did. As the two of us were having a delightful breakfast and conversation my clients began coming in for breakfast and had surprised looks on their faces as they passed. Dalitz and I never discussed the Teamsters, financing or his past. Nor did I ever ask him for a favor. Not one of my clients asked me about him. And I had absolutely superb service the rest of my stay and on future visits to La Costa.

Chapter 13

Organize For Success

Throughout my career I have been fortunate to have several mentors who taught me much about business in general and especially the public relations profession. You can learn a great deal from mentors that you will never learn in college. Always remember to give back and help others because regardless of your level of experience what you do know can be of help to someone else.

My mentors emphasized that being organized is critical to success. If more people organized and prioritized, fewer would use "busy" as an excuse for not getting a job done or not doing it on time. Unfortunately, too many do not practice self-discipline and the word deadline is not part of their vocabulary. Following is my definition of busy:

> **busy** (bi-zee), adj., 1) an individual's relative state of being that is dependent on his or her ability (or inability) to organize one's self; 2) a most overused word given as an excuse for not performing a task; 3) often used as an excuse by procrastinators; 4) all too often a function of creating unnecessary work in order to appear productive.

Today we live in an age of information and electronic technology. We have scores of electronic devices to help organize our lives.

I do not believe we will never be a paperless society – lawyers make sure of that. Good organization is important in whatever you do. Organize your time. Manage your time. Know how you spend your time. Keep good records and use systems that work best for you.

To Do List

One of my early mentors, Bob Williams at Lennen & Newell, encouraged me to do a daily "to do" list. At the end of the work day I listed and prioritized what needed to be done the next day including phone calls, memos, letters, projects, and meetings. The list can be kept on a computer or written out. Before I retired I needed a legal-sized yellow ruled pad. Even in retirement I make a daily list and today I use just a 5"x7" pad. Don't worry if you can't finish everything on the list. That starts tomorrow's "to do" list.

Keep A Telephone Log

I believe it is important to record all incoming and outgoing calls, the date, the time, and disposition of the call. Did you talk to the person and what was the subject? Did you leave a message with the secretary or a voice mail? Was the line busy? Telephone logs are an easy way to stay organized. You can refer to your log when a person challenges you about not returning a call and you can give that person the time(s) and date(s) when you attempted to return the call or left word that you had called. Most telephone calls today can be tracked but it is important to have a log if needed for any legal purposes.

Follow-Up File

Bob Williams taught me a simple system that is an easy reminder when any particular action is needed. Many electronic devices can organize this for you but I prefer the old fashioned way by taking 31 file folders numbered 1 through 31. I keep them in a file drawer and place items in the appropriate file on the dates when I want to be reminded of a needed action. Some are hand written notes as a reminder to call someone or do something in so many days. I keep copies of letters and other memos by placing a copy in the file "x" days from the date it was written, as a reminder to see if a follow up second request is needed. Determine the length of time you want for a response or for action and then place your correspondence or note in the date of that file folder.

Once your follow-up file system is in place check it daily. Occasionally you may forget that a particular date is a Saturday, Sunday or holiday so be sure to check the files ahead of those days.

There are software programs that will allow you to set up such a follow-up system on your computer, but not for odd sizes of hard copies unless you scan and digitize them. Just do what works best for you.

Keep Copies

There will be times you may want to make an extra copy of a letter so one can be in an action file and the other in your follow-up file and available if ever needed. In a competitive environment there is the possibility that for whatever reason you cannot trust a business colleague. Copy even a handwritten note, keep it in a safe place and even give a copy to a friend. If a person would lie about receiving a note or memo, that person probably will not think that anyone would keep a file copy of a handwritten note. With email you can blind copy a friend. More than once during my career having copied a friend has been like having money in the bank.

Bob Williams thought I was not being given credit by a co-worker for my ideas and might even blame me for his mistakes. In the days before email, Bob had me copy him on certain memos and handwritten notes that he kept in a special file.
This process worked and saved my job. A fellow employee made a serious mistake that nearly lost a client. I thought he was a friend but later discovered I could not trust him. This was confirmed when he lied to Bob saying "… the mistake was "Rene's fault." Bob reached into his desk and pulled out a copy of one of my notes from the special file, confronted the employee, and fired him on the spot. I went home that night thinking how I could have been the one cleaning out my desk.

Organize For Success | 119

Document Dates For Information

The U.S. Postal Service is an inexpensive way to document when information was sent to a person. The routine way is to send a letter certified or registered with a return receipt and to deliver to addressee only. This doesn't always work because in large offices someone in the mail room will sign for all mail. Often that individual's signature will be illegible and you cannot always prove the contents of the letter.

If you have an idea you want to protect make a copy and put it in an envelope addressed and mailed to yourself. Code the envelope so you know its contents and put the document in a safe place in case you ever need it to resolve a problem. Do not open it until it is necessary. Depending on the importance of the document you can always mail it to yourself certified so it is tracked by the USPS.

Budget Management

Whether it is personal, for a company or organization, or client, budget management is very important. I have used several different types of budgets. The most basic is just that – a list of items on the left with a cost estimate in a column on the right. People commonly use a budget balance for the financial status of a project and this is simply three columns of the original budget, the money spent and the balance remaining.

The budget I prefer is taking the budget balance with committed funds by adding two additional columns on the right. One will show the unspent amount that is committed or estimated to be spent at a later date and the final column the balance after that deduction. This prevents someone from spending money today without realizing those funds will be needed in subsequent weeks or months.

Another budget I favor is one that details the cash flow of expenses. Following the column of the budget, other columns will detail weekly or monthly when that line item will be spent. I also like a combination of this budget and the one above. All you have to do is add the commitment column and final balance. Both of these allow for more detailed planning without any surprises.

Table 19.3. Budget balance

Line Item	Budget ($)	Spent ($)	Balance ($)
1.0 Press releases			
1.1 Production and mailing	3,500.00	1,542.36	1,957.64
1.2 Distribution service	8,500.00	5,355.75	3,144.25
1.3 VNRs	12,000.00	6,126.17	5,873.83
2.0 Photography/graphics			
2.1 Photography	4,000.00	3,228.94	771.06
2.2 Graphics/logos design	7,500.00	8,755.44	(1,255.44)
2.3 Quantity prints	2,500.00	1,685.25	814.75
3.0 Postage, messenger and delivery services	3,000.00	1,942.63	1,057.37
4.0 Telephone and fax	5,000.00	3,112.37	1,887.63
5.0 Press conferences (2 cities)	10,000.00	9,847.81	152.19
6.0 Special events (TBA)	10,000.00	4,789.34	5,210.66
7.0 Travel and per diem	15,000.00	9,891.47	5,108.53
8.0 Results measurement			
8.1 Clipping service	4,000.00	2,341.96	1,658.04
8.2 Audio/video monitoring	3,000.00	2,246.87	753.13
Sub-total	88,000.00	60,866.36	27,133.64
9.0 10% contingency	8,800.00	—0—	8,800.00
Total	96,800.00	60,866.36	35,933.64

Communicate

Until the era of spam, junk mail and unsolicited robocalled phone calls, I had a policy to return every phone call and answer every letter, memo, fax and email. I have had a practice for years to not screen calls and have not allowed employees to have someone else screen or place calls for them. I believe anyone who works for an organization supported by public tax dollars should always be accessible no matter who is calling or why. A public servant whose salary is paid for by tax dollars has the responsibility to respond and especially be available for the media.

In several of my jobs I always received unsolicited résumés and calls by vendors wanting to sell something. I answered all and in the case of job seekers made an effort to personalize my response. Over the years several people called me to thank me and one even retained my firm because of my responsiveness.

It is not always possible to return all calls. Smart business people I know will have a secretary or assistant return a call if s/he is delayed in a meeting or out of town. Ask the importance of the call and whether it should be returned in the evening at the caller's residence. When time demands prevent returning all calls promptly, have a secretary or assistant phone the callers to let them know, starting in the Eastern time zone first, then Midwest and move to the Pacific time zone.

As a matter of good business practice, telephone calls should be returned within 24 hours, faxes, emails and letters should be acknowledged or answered with 72 hours.

If you are going to be on travel leave an out-of-town or vacation response on your email to send an automatic reply to a sender. Voicemails should be updated as well. Some people update their voicemails every week and some even every day.

Time Management

There is more waste, inefficiency and mismanagement today because few people know how to properly manage their time. Too many people don't have a clue as to how long it takes to perform a certain task or how to account for how their day was spent. Professional service organizations including attorneys, accountants, architects and those in public relations and other disciplines keep records for billing purposes. Some bill to the nearest quarter-hour, but most law firms have time sheets to the one-tenth of an hour, or in increments of six minutes.

When I was an individual practitioner I kept a time sheet for self-discipline. I wanted to see if I was giving appropriate attention to my clients and it was critical for billing special projects for clients. However, some people just cannot keep time sheets. They either have a mental block or fear of taking responsibility for their actions. At ICPR we wanted to withhold giving a paycheck until the time sheet was turned in but this was considered an unfair labor practice. However, it was a point made during salary reviews. When I was executive director of university relations at Texas A&M, I initiated the keeping of time sheets much to the chagrin of some of my staff. I structured my office to function as a full service marketing communications agency.

The people who most needed to keep time sheets and to be accountable and responsible for their time were the ones who most resisted the process. Even after several years a couple of employees never turned their time sheets in on time or understood the meaning of a deadline. One senior level manager never had a deadline she didn't like because she never finished a project on time even when I let her set her own deadline. I do not believe she ever was on time to one of our weekly staff meetings and she gave a new meaning to the word procrastinate.

At A&M I also began using a PERT chart[24] to ensure that a product was delivered on time and on budget. To best manage a project or campaign put all of the information on a chart such as the one below which is a simplified example. List all of the major projects and sub-projects on the left and when they are due with a schedule of weeks (or days or months) at the top. The more detailed the timeline the better. Months can be broken down by weeks. Keys can be used to assign individual responsibility for each line item. Following is a simplified example that can be further detailed by weeks.

Table 19.2. Campaign production schedule

Project	Jan	Feb	Mar	Apr	May	Jun	Jul	Aug	Sep	Oct	Nov	Dec	Jan	Feb
1. Design letterhead, logo, materials	/——/													
2. Interview and select spokesperson		/——/												
3. Prepare press kit materials				/——/										
4. Press conferences														
Advance, finalize arrangements					/-/									
New York						/-/								
Atlanta						/-/								
Dallas							/-/							
Los Angeles							/-/							
5. Special events														
Advance, finalize arrangements							/-/							
Concert							/-/							
10K bicycle event									/-/					
6. Distribute news releases, as appropriate			/——————————————————————/											
7. Prepare, distribute video news releases							/-/		/-/		/-/		/-/	
8. Report on media results				/——————————————————/										
9. Research														
Precampaign		/——/												
Campaign evaluation													/——/	

With a project time/line chart like the one above any person can instantly see if a project is ahead of or behind schedule and make adjustments accordingly. This helps keeps individuals responsible

---

24 A PERT chart is a project management tool used to schedule, organize and coordinate tasks. It stands for Program Evaluation Review Technique, a methodology developed by the U.S. Navy in the 1950s to manage the Polaris submarine missile program. A similar methodology is the Critical Path Method (CPM) that was developed for project management in the private sector at about the same time.

and accountable for certain tasks. If some individuals spend more time than estimated and allocated for a particular function, then in the real world it could mean taking a loss on the job.

Good time management results in increased productivity, efficiency and quality of product. Tailor any time management system to best work for you and your office. It doesn't cost anything to be well organized. And it will pay big dividends and rewards.

Chapter 14

How Mo Mo Saved My Life

Norman Moomjian was a classmate at William & Mary where his friends called him Mo Mo. He became a successful restaurateur and his Copain restaurant in New York City was always highly rated by the critics. It was located on First Avenue near the United Nations and adjacent to tony Sutton Place.

Every time I was in New York I dined at Copain at least one night or stopped by for a nightcap. The bar was like Cheer's and frequented by those in the neighborhood. One regular was Jack Molinas, a basketball All-American at Columbia, a professional in the National Basketball Association, and a lawyer. He was very intelligent, extremely personable, charismatic, a great story teller, and considered the greatest fixer of basketball games in history. He is one of the most interesting characters I have met.

Jack The Fixer

In his book, *The Wizard of Odds*, Charley Rosen says Molinas nearly destroyed the game of basketball. He had a genius IQ of 175 and was in an elite group when he was one of the youngest to ever pass the New York State Bar exam. He did so his first time which only half of the future lawyers do. He grew up in a middle-class Jewish family in the Bronx and began both his basketball and gambling career as a teenager at Stuyvesant High School in Manhattan. Molinas badly missed a free throw in the city championship game won by Abraham Lincoln 41-40. He later said he threw the game for $800.[25]

At 6'6" and 200 pounds, in 1951 he led Columbia to one of its most successful seasons with a 22-0 record and #3 ranking in the country. In many of the 59 games Molinas played for the Ivy League Lions he shaved points and made sure his gambler friends beat the point spread. He shared in their winnings. He graduated with academic and athletic honors in 1953 and was the #1 draft choice of the Ft. Wayne Zollner Pistons with a $9,600 contract and a $500 signing bonus. As a rookie he was named to the NBA All-Star game but was suspended on January 10, 1954 after 29 games when he admitted he placed bets on his team.

When he was only 12 years old Molinas made his first bet with a local bookie. It was on the Yankees and he lost. But his new friend taught him all about odds, point spreads and vigorish[26].

His suspension was only a part of the college basketball gambling scandal. New York District Attorney Frank Hogan indicted players from four New York City colleges, including seven from CCNY, a team that accomplished one of the great feats in basketball winning both the NCAA and NIT tournaments the year before. Eventually 32 players from seven colleges were arrested along with gamblers and fixers.[27]

$10,000 a Year vs. $50,000 a Week

Molinas quickly realized that he could only make $10,000 a year playing professional basketball but he could recruit student-athletes to manipulate the scores of games for $1,000 a night and then sell

---

25 Charley Rosen, *The Wizard of Odds – How Jack Molinas Almost Destroyed the Game of Basketball*, Seven Stories Press, New York, N.Y., 2001

26 According to Wikipedia, vigorish, or the vig, is the amount charged by a bookmaker for taking a bet. It also is called juice, under-juice, the cut or the take. It also means the interest paid to a loan shark.

27 Charley Rosen, *op.cit.*

the fixed game to a bookmaker for $10,000. He would bet several thousand dollars of his own money on the game and clear $50,000 a week.

According to sports writer Neil D. Isaacs, Molinas was both a compulsive gambler and scam artist. He had a boxer drugged to fix a fight. He tried to fix horse races using a remote electric buzzer that would give a motivational jolt to the butt of a horse. He even was able to manipulate the clocks in back-room betting parlors by getting a friend at Con Edison to reduce the electricity feed. With the clocks a minute later than when race began, Molinas could bet on horses that had already won races. A brilliant individual, while he was in prison he even was involved in a scheme using a signature machine to forge checks.[28]

Between 1957 and 1961, Molinas rigged the outcomes of at least 43 basketball games involving 476 players at 27 colleges and leading to the arrests of 37 players. When he was arrested in January 1962, he was considered the mastermind of the scandal. On February 11, 1963, he was sentenced to prison for 10 to 15 years and served five, mostly at the Attica, New York Correctional Facility.[29]

The colleges involved included Columbia, NYU, North Carolina, N.C. State, Seton Hall, LaSalle, St. John's, Utah, Bowling Green, Alabama, College of the Pacific, and St. Joseph's of Philadelphia. He recruited many of the players he befriended on New York playgrounds during the summers and when they were in high school[30].

One evening at the Copain bar he told me how media exposure led to his arrest. He wanted to be sure things went as planned when the College of the Pacific played St. Mary's College in Moraga, California. "There were many empty seats so I took one high up near the top and in the dark. No one was around me," he said. "And then I heard a voice say 'Jacob… Jacob Molinas, is that you

---

28 Ibid.
29 Ibid.
30 Ibid.

my son?' It was the parish priest from my old neighborhood in the Bronx! At halftime, he told everyone at the press table that I was in the area, that I wanted to see the game and that I was one of the greatest basketball players ever. The story was in the *San Francisco Chronicle* the next day.

"An FBI agent read the item and remembered me from 10 years before. He heard that the New York district attorney was looking into college basketball gambling," he continued. "One thing led to another and soon it was all over."

Sometimes the fixed games didn't go always as Molinas planned. Another night he told me that some bookies and gamblers had lost thousands of dollars on his word and wanted pay back. This led to two thugs holding him by his ankles outside a 40-story window of a New York hotel. This incident was a fictionalized scene in the movie *The Godfather*.

The Move To Los Angeles

In the early 1970s he moved to Los Angeles and co-founded a company that produced and distributed pornographic movies. When I would see him at Copain he always asked me to call him and stop by his Hollywood Hills home on a weekend and relax by the pool. In 1974, Jack collected a $500,000 life insurance policy when his business partner Bernard Gusoff was beaten to death. I was unaware of this.[31]

In 1975, the atmosphere of Copain had changed. The restaurant no longer was filled to capacity with diners. The usual neighborhood crowd no longer was at the bar. Instead there was a mean-looking, mobster-type sitting at the end of the bar by the cash register. Central Casting couldn't have picked a better stereotype and I would bet that he was carrying a gun. He always had a couple of his goodfellow cronies around. Norm Moomjian, who had a penchant for gambling, was no longer was running his restaurant.

In late September 1975, Jack invited me to his house one Saturday afternoon for a casual party. I accepted. Two days later

---
31 Ibid.

my friend Mo Mo called from New York. "Rene, listen. Don't say a word. I'm telling you this just once. Stay away from Jack," he said. "If he invites you to a party at his house, do not go. I'll tell you why the next time I see you. But remember, stay away from Jack." He then hung up.

The next evening while listening to the 11 p.m. news my heart was in my throat when I heard the newscaster say, "Tonight former basketball star Jack Molinas was murdered gangland style in his Hollywood Hills home." I was in a state of shock and thought how I could have been there had it not been for Mo Mo's call. In his book, Rosen suggests that it was a mob-directed hit because of several unpaid debts. The murder remains unsolved.

I never got the full story from Mo Mo. Several weeks after this incident, Richie, the Copain bartender, called to tell me my friend died of a gunshot wound to the head in his apartment above the restaurant. The police called it a suicide. I doubt it.

How Mo Mo Saved My Life | 129

Chapter 15

Memorable Moments

I have been very lucky to be at the right place at the right time for what have been historic moments in my life. By far, my most memorable and joyful moments were at St. Mary's Hospital in San Francisco when my daughter Deborah was born and at Marin General Hospital in San Rafael when my son Bruce was born.

I could write volumes about the wonderful loving memories I've had with my children, my parents, my family, friends and pets. They are the most precious of all memories.

World War II

In 1937 before my father passed away I would sit next to him as he listened to the news on the radio. He was especially concerned about the rise of Hitler and the Nazis because of our family roots and relatives in Belgium.

Four years later when I came out of a movie theater a newspaper boy was yelling: "Extra, extra, read all about it. Japs bomb Pearl Harbor." It wasn't until I got home that I learned where Pearl Harbor was and how what happened would shape history and impact my family. Newspapers published extra editions in those days and the sources of news were newspapers and the radio.

Soon I was participating in patriotic parades and events to

honor and support our troops. I had a little red wagon I pulled around the neighborhood to collect scrap metal for the war effort.

My grandmother regularly sent essential items to her family in Nazi-occupied Belgium. They had to be contained in a large cloth bound stitch-sealed ball. I helped her carry these to the post office. She showed me letters from her family with sentences and sometimes entire paragraphs blacked by Nazi censors.

In the summer of 1942 when I was visiting my aunt, uncle and cousin in Glenwood Landing I remember looking up and seeing the sky filled with convoys of airplanes flying to Britain. The bombers were flying in formation the way birds migrate today. The convoys seemed endless. PT boats[32] like the one skippered by John F. Kennedy were being built nearby and we could see them tested at full speed in the adjacent bay.

9/11

On September 11, 2001 I was in my EPA office in Philadelphia when a colleague ran in and asked me to turn on my television. He said a plane had crashed into a World Trade Center tower in New York. I was one of the few people in EPA that had a TV set. Soon there were a dozen or more people in the room when we watched in horror as a second plane crashed into the adjacent tower.

I had a meeting scheduled the next day at the Pentagon City Marriott. While we listened to the news I called to see if the conference was still scheduled. A panicked hotel operator answered. I heard bells and sirens going off in the background. All she could say, nearly screaming hysterically, was "I don't know…I don't know…I have to go."

I said to those in my room that in a few minutes we're going to hear tragic news about something that happened at The Pentagon. In less than a half hour we learned of the third hijacked plane crash.

---

32 PT stands for Patrol Torpedo, a small, fast, very maneuverable U.S. Navy attack boat armed with torpedoes and inexpensive to build.

The First Prize

All through elementary and junior high school I don't remember ever winning anything. I would get some awards and honors, but not the first prize, blue ribbon. During my junior year in high school at the annual awards assembly I applauded for my classmates and friends as they accepted various awards. Then I heard the principal announce "Rene Henry, first place in Virginia for sports writing!" I was in disbelief until he announced it a second time and my classmates were nudging and congratulating me to go to the stage and receive the award.

I was the sports editor of the school newspaper and unaware of a Quill & Scroll Society contest judged at the Medill School of Journalism at Northwestern University. I'm glad my teacher/advisor submitted one of my articles. I was so excited about the honor I ran all the way home to tell my parents the news. And, I was lucky to win the same first prize again my senior year.

Stardust In French Lick, Indiana

During the 1971 Republican Governors Conference I had a couple of drinks one afternoon with songwriter/composer Hoagy Carmichael. Then that evening during the gala dinner I watched as he played and sang "Stardust." You could have heard a pin drop in the room. Jim Price, the chairman and CEO of National Homes Corporation in Lafayette, Indiana, retained me to help present a modular housing demonstration during the conference.

Hollywood At Its Best

The most lavish and extravagant Hollywood party I attended was organized by my partners for a studio preview of *At Long Last Love* in March 1975. It probably was one of the most expensive. Our client was 20th Century-Fox. Director/Screenwriter Peter Bogdanovich was then involved with 25-year-old Cybil Shepherd who he cast in the leading role. The elegant party after the screening was right out of a movie but critics panned the film that featured the songs of Cole Porter.

A soundstage duplicated the grandeur of Pasadena's Huntington Hartford Hotel in the 1930s. George Hamilton welcomed the arriving guests at the top of a grand staircase. Liza Minnelli and Lorna Luft were just two of the entertainers.

My partners worked almost to party time changing table seating arrangements each time there was an acceptance or regret. I went quickly from an "A" table hosted by Fox's chairman and CEO, Dennis Stanfill and his wife Terry, to no table. Rita Hayworth, one of Hollywood's top stars of the 1940s and 1950s, accepted but wanted a date. Without asking me, my partners told me I would escort her and make sure she did not drink too much or create a scene. She was then 57. She died 12 years later of Alzheimer's, a recluse, and the opposite of the glamorous and sexy roles she played. Glenn Ford, her next door neighbor, told me she was reputed to be a heavy drinker. I got to know him several years earlier when he hosted a celebrity wine tasting at his home for my client, the California Wine Institute.

While the "blind date" could have been an experience, I did not look forward to the exposure, media coverage or my responsibility for the evening. Late Saturday afternoon she cancelled. I thoroughly enjoyed the evening.

Black Tie Garage Sale

One of the most fun Hollywood parties I attended was in the late 1970s when Carol Burnett had an invitation only, elegant black-tie garage sale. She and her husband Joe Hamilton were moving to a new house in Beverly Hills that she was having redecorated. The auction was held on their spacious back lawn where guests were served champagne, hors d'oeuvres, and a great buffet dinner following the auction.

We were given numbered paddles to bid with and toured the house to see the various items being sold. Supporting the professional auctioneers were Tim Conway and Harvey Korman who had everyone rolling in the aisles with their antics.

Flying High

One of my best commercial flying experiences was riding in the cockpit of a 747 from Perth to Sydney, Australia. I had been in Perth for Burson-Marsteller for the 1987 America's Cup yacht race in Freemantle to package a number of pre-race events for television. Our client, Ray O'Connor, was the former premier of Western Australia who served 25 years in Parliament. He treated me royally during my nearly two weeks in Perth. He personally saw me off for my flight home and I was given the VIP treatment.

During the Qantas flight the captain invited me to join him in the cockpit after dinner. I've never had a flight like that since! I didn't return for the race but watched on television as Dennis Connor, sailing Stars & Stripes, reclaimed the Cup for the U.S. beating Australia's 12-meter Kookaburra III.

Le Cordon Bleu

For a long time one of my wish list items was cooking lessons at Le Cordon Bleu in Paris. I had no idea what to expect when I visited the world famous school, not for classes, but for a client, Magic Pan Restaurants, who was giving a contest winner an all-expense paid week of cooking classes, air fare and hotel. I was surprised that it was in a plain, small store front in a nondescript section of the city. I met with Madam Élisabeth Brassart who ran the school from 1945 to 1984, retiring when she was 87 years old. She was unfavorably portrayed in Julia Child's biography. The film Julie & Julia caricatured her to dramatize an incident that Child wrote about and others have repeated. It certainly does not properly represent most people's memory of her. I found her extremely charming, delightful and most accommodating.

A Belgian friend who drove me to my appointments and handled translation situations told Madam Brassart that I had neglected to make dinner reservations that evening. At many of the best Parisian restaurants it is essential to do so days and sometimes weeks in advance. She smiled and said "Do not worry. I trained all of the best chefs." She made a couple of suggestions, asked what time we wanted to dine, made one call and we dined exquisitely that evening.

The Only Way To See The White House

In high school I was part of a tour group that had a chance to walk through public areas of the White House. Ropes prevented you from touching any furniture. As the tour guide led us through the various rooms I never thought I would ever return as a guest. On September 27, 1974 I was an official delegate to President Ford's Conference On Inflation and that included a White House reception.

What a thrill it was walking in the entrance and with other delegates being welcomed by President and Mrs. Ford. I could walk freely from the East Room to the State Dining Room and through the Green, Blue and Red Rooms off the Cross Hall. I mingled with the nation's leaders of business and industry and cabinet officials and enjoyed drinks and hors d'oeuvres. During the afternoon session that day I had the good fortune to sit next to and talk with George Meany, the head of the AFL-CIO and probably the nation's most important labor leader. I still have the pin he put on my lapel that reads "The Problem Is More Than Inflation."

A decade later I had meetings in the West Wing; dined in the White House Mess; coordinated a promotional video for state Republican conventions that starred President George H.W. and Mrs. Bush and was filmed just off the Rose Garden; and was a member of the official party when the 1984 U.S. Olympic Team was hosted on the South Lawn. I'm still waiting for another social invitation on the State Second Floor!

Winning The Gold

Beginning in 1968 I worked to seek the Olympic Games for Los Angeles in 1976 and 1980 and again 1984, so in May 1978 in Athens, Greece, it was a wonderful experience to hear Lord Killanin, president of the International Olympic Committee, announced Los Angeles would be the site of the 1984 Olympic Games. Hours, days and weeks of volunteer work in the preceding months paid off. It was an eventful week in Athens leading to the selection.

The following day U.S. Ambassador to Greece, Robert McCloskey, and his wife Anne graciously hosted our delegation at their residence to celebrate. Long before there was Benghazi many in our diplomatic corps had safety concerns. Mrs. McCloskey pointed out three exits from their walled residence, all on different streets, that were used when leaving their Athens home. In recent years U.S. ambassadors had been assassinated in Cyprus and Lebanon and she said her husband's two-car caravan always used a different exit and route each day.

Know The Language

I learned the importance of knowing a foreign language the previous evening. I was with Mayor Tom Bradley, Deputy Mayor Anton Calleia, Bea Lavery the city's chief of protocol, TV Producer David Wolper, and Hank Rieger, NBC vice president of public relations, as we made several stops to celebrate.

Following a stop at the Soviet Embassy, we went to the Yugoslavian Embassy to toast Sarajevo as the host for the 1984 Olympic Winter Games. After all of the introductions and toasts I needed to find a bathroom. I was pointed in the general direction and asked a security guard in English with no response. French brought no response. Finally, I asked in Spanish and he directed the way. I found it interesting that Spanish was a common language in the Yugoslavian Embassy in Greece but then remembered that Cuba was a favorite vacation site for the Soviets and their allies.

Foreign language has never been one of my strengths but having spent considerable time in Mexico I do get by in Spanish. I've learned Italian three times and it has served me well but I forget it within a week of returning home. My French was passable when I was involved in Olympic and international sports.

An associate of mine learned the importance of knowing a foreign language in 1985 when we were staying at a small hotel in Dueville, Italy to attend the World Cycling Championships in nearby Bassano del Grappa. Only the owner knew enough English to carry on a conversation. We all had different schedules and didn't always dine together every morning. On the fourth day several of us were having a full breakfast with ham, eggs, toast, fruit, juice and coffee or tea when my language-illiterate colleague arrived and was excited when he saw what we were eating. "How did you get a breakfast like that?" he asked. "All I've been able to get for breakfast is a Coca-Cola and bag of chips." I said the hotel had no menu and all you had to do was ask the cook to prepare what you wanted. He began speaking English to the young woman who didn't understand a word he said. "All you need to do is politely tell her what you want in Italian," I said. I relented and ordered breakfast for him.

When I was in Morocco and street vendors were aggressively trying to sell items to tourists many in my group just brushed them aside but I made a point to politely say, "No, merci." Then one peddler asked me in French if I was Canadian and when I responded that I was American he looked at me in disbelief and said "No, no, not possible. Canadian." That only reinforces what we hear about Americans being rude and arrogant.

Wherever I am in the world I try to learn some of the basic phrases – please, thank you, you're welcome, excuse me, and especially where to find the bathroom. In China I also needed to learn the characters. When you travel internationally I believe it is important to make every effort to learn the language and know the local social customs dos and don'ts.

Feeling Completely Helpless

One time I realized I probably should have learned Flemish or Dutch. My friends who lived in The Netherlands and Belgium told me that everyone was multilingual in both countries. I assumed French and English would get me by. One day it did not.

I was visiting my friends Wies Andersen and Monique Moritz in Brasschaat, Belgium, a suburb of Antwerp. He was a movie star and had the country's #1 rated TV show. She was a magazine journalist and a TV news commentator. I wanted to sightsee Antwerp and the first day Wies dropped me off in town he first showed me where to get the bus to return home. This worked perfectly for two days. The bus stop was at the end of their long driveway.

The third day just a few blocks before where I wanted to get off, the bus made a strange turn. I thought perhaps it would turn back to the main street but before I knew it, we were out of town heading in a new direction. I tried to communicate with the driver but he did not speak English, French, Spanish or Italian. Only Flemish. It was the same with a handful of passengers on the bus.

I was ready to panic and looking for a place to get off to call Wies but then realized at a pay telephone I wouldn't be able to tell him where I was. This was before the days of cellphones. Finally, I saw an area with a couple of restaurants so I got off. I walked up the driveway to one and soon realized it was too early for it to be open. As I was leaving, a woman opened the door and asked in French what I wanted. I told her I was lost, showed her Wies' business card and asked her to please call him and tell him where I was. She broke into a big smile, welcomed me inside, and gave me a glass of wine while she phoned him.

We returned to the restaurant that night and the woman showed us a picture of her and Wies as young children. Their parents were friends. Wies told me it soon became one of his favorite restaurants. He kidded me about coming all the way from Los Angeles to find a great restaurant for him!

How Do You Say That In Spanish?

I spent two weeks in Santiago, Chile consulting the Chilean Government on housing issues ranging from manufactured housing and wood frame design to building standards and mortgage financing. Several days I met with Chile's Council of Economic Advisors that was headed by a Ph.D. graduate from Cal-Berkeley who was fluent in English. All of the others were disciplines of the University of Chicago's Milton Friedman.

One afternoon I was discussing the workings of a secondary mortgage market and the chair was late. I was explaining the profit structure on bonds when interest payment is received monthly and dividends are paid quarterly, semi-annually or annually and this became what is called the float.

I had a dozen people in a room looking at me puzzled who did not understand my explanation. Finally, the chairman arrived and I told him I was trying to explain float. He smiled at me and then told his colleagues. They then all responded Ah Ha!

My Friend Hot Rod

I met Rod Hundley in March 1954 during the Southern Conference basketball tournament in Morgantown. Just a couple of months later I was the sports information director at West Virginia University and part of my job was to promote him for All-American honors. Better known as Hot Rod, he made my job easy. On December 28, 1954 he put on one of the greatest shooting exhibitions I have seen when he scored 47 points in a losing cause 96-94 against Wake Forest in the Dixie Classic in Raleigh, N.C. It was a record for both the tournament and the arena.

A week later, he scored 37 points for a Madison Square Garden record but WVU lost 79-78 to New York University. Rod and I regularly kept in touch for more than 60 years and stayed connected often when our travel schedules had us both in the same city. His terrible affliction with Alzheimer's made it impossible to for us to communicate the last few months of his life.

An All-American, in three years and in only 89 games he scored 2,180 points and is the only Mountaineer to be drafted #1 in any professional sport. He played six years with the Minneapolis and later Los Angeles Lakers, twice making the All-Star team. He became a Hall of Fame sportscaster, was the voice of the Utah Jazz for 35 years, and broadcast more than 3,500 basketball games. He invited me to be in Morgantown when his #33 was retired. For a perfect ending, dressed in a suit and tie and street shoes, he made a 15' hook shot. Alzheimer's took him from us on March 27, 2015. The only other Mountaineer to have his number retired and to score more career points is another friend and basketball legend, Jerry West.

January 9, 1958, I saw another great break Hundley's Madison Square Garden record when Oscar Robertson scored 56 points to lead Cincinnati to a 118-54 win over Seton Hall. Yogi Berra and Joe Garagiola sat in front of me and were outraged when coach Ed Jucker substituted for Robertson with a couple of minutes left in the game so he could get a standing ovation. They yelled "That's like pulling Babe Ruth out of a game when he has a chance to hit five home runs! Let him score 60 points!

Steve Allen – A Remarkable Individual

Steve Allen was a television personality, musician, composer, actor, comedian, and writer who launched *The Tonight Show*. He was a basketball fan, was at Madison Square Garden to see Hundley's scoring feat and even stopped by the WVU dressing room after the game to offer his congratulations. That afternoon, before the game, I tried unsuccessfully to convince his producers to have Hundley appear as a guest on his show that night. They obviously didn't know Allen that well.

In the late 60s Allen hosted a syndicated TV show out of Burbank. I knew his producer and we worked together on a number of projects for my clients that included a California wine tasting; providing his wardrobe from Michaels-Stern; interviewing a handwriting expert for Paper Mate Pens; discussing citrus-colored clothes with a spokeswoman for Sunkist; and taking a bath in Quaker Oats oatmeal. When Kimberly-Clark introduced paper clothes we had a bikini specially made so Allen could pull out tissues without exposing the model. We had a great working relationship.

Then 20 years later when I was in federal service and on an awards committee I was asked to find a celebrity to make the presentations. We had no budget for any honorarium. Allen was on stage in Washington. I called him and he graciously accepted and made the day.

A Nationwide Olympic Celebration

My most challenging special event, as well as one of the most rewarding, was the week-long tour of the 1984 U.S. Olympic medal winners. Underwritten by client Southland/7-Eleven, every U.S. medal winner could invite a guest. The tour began Monday morning, August 13 in Los Angeles at a breakfast with President Ronald Reagan and attended by local civic leaders and government officials.

The next stop was Washington, D.C. where several thousand people were at Dulles airport when our three chartered 727s arrived late in the evening. The Tuesday event at the Capitol drew thousands more. Then on to New York where the police blocked all traffic from JFK airport to Manhattan for the 12-bus motorcade. Traffic was backed up for miles on the Grand Central Parkway but fans were out of their cars, waving American flags and shouting, "USA, USA." More fans lined the bus route from the Queens Midtown Tunnel to the Plaza Hotel. Because of the Soviet boycott and success of the U.S. Olympians, patriotism was never higher.

Rafer Johnson, Olympic gold decathlon champion in 1960 who lit the flame to start the Los Angeles Games, Don Smith, and I were in the last bus in the convoy. We were choked up with emotion from the response. Don and I co-produced the event. The next day more than two-and-one-half million people lined Broadway to salute the Olympians. Mayor Ed Koch led the parade flanked by gymnasts Mary Lou Retton and Julianne MacNamara. It was the largest ticker-tape parade in New York City history until the one that honored the veterans returning from Desert Storm.

Following speeches and tributes at City Hall, it was on to Orlando, Florida where the Olympians and guests enjoyed Disneyworld before a final stop in Dallas on Friday. The largest crowd for a Dallas parade welcomed the athletes, and a barbecue at Southfork Ranch, complete with fireworks, capped the week-long event.

On May 8, 1984, the Soviets announced it would not participate. Cuba, East Germany and 14 Eastern Bloc countries followed.

This created a challenge for us to predict the number of medal winners who would be on the tour. Don and I spent days researching each of the 23 sports, talking to athletes and coaches, and counted the number of Olympians on teams as well as individuals who might win several medals. We came up with a number of 225 medal winners or a total 450 with guests. We anticipated not all medal winners would be on the tour every day of the week. We had the right numbers for the airplane charters, hotel reservations and budget. Don and I met with many of the teams before the Games to let them know of our plans. Southland's own travel office did a fantastic job coordinating arrangements for the guests to start the tour and for all returning home from Dallas.

Stars And A Stripe

I was on active military duty assigned to the athletic department at the U.S. Military Academy at West Point when it hosted the first meeting of the President's Council On Physical Fitness & Sports, September 9-10, 1957. The year before this assignment I had met Col. George Creel and he asked that I be assigned to him for the conference.

A week before following a pre-season football game of the New York Giants I had been with superstar Frank Gifford and Edwin Mosler, CEO of the Mosler Safe Co. Frank asked me to be sure and give his best to Vice President Richard M. Nixon, who was chairing the meeting. Mosler also was a member of the council.

When it was appropriate I walked to the Vice President and gave him Frank's best. During the pre-season, the team was staying at nearby Bear Mountain Lodge and he said I would be doing him a personal favor if I could get Frank to meet him in his hotel suite before he left West Point. Frank came with Don Heinrich, the Giants' backup quarterback, and joined Ed Mosler and me and the four of us went to Nixon's suite.

After a few minutes Nixon asked me to get a photographer to take a picture of him with the football stars. When I got off the elevator in the lobby to find a photographer the head of public relations for the USMA, a colonel said the meeting was causing a delay with all of the brass waiting to say goodbye. Back in the suite the photograph was taken and Nixon continued the conversation with all of us. Twice his aide reminded him a reception party was waiting for him in the lobby and that he was running late. Nixon said he would be ready in due time.

When Nixon, his aide, Gifford, Heinrich, Mosler and I, in uniform with my one private first class stripe, stepped off the elevator there were indeed two lines of Army brass waiting to pay their respects. I couldn't help but see their faces when Nixon took my hand and said, "Rene, thank you so very much. We'll be in touch soon."

I coordinated getting signatures on the photographs for everyone and indeed we were meeting again soon. This time it was the annual dinner of the New York Baseball Writers' Association. Nixon was the featured speaker and Mosler had a table that was front and center. I was his guest along with other sports notables including Boston Celtics' basketball Hall of Famer Bob Cousey; baseball All-Star Bobby Thomson who is best known for his home run when the Giants beat the Dodgers for the National League Pennant in 1951; New York Knicks' coach Red Holzman, and others.

When Nixon came out and saw Mosler and me he made a point to to greet us. I couldn't help but notice but several rows back the West Point athletic department and brass had a table and again gave me looks that could kill.

Goodbye Polo Grounds

On Sunday September 28, 1957, I watched the New York Giants split a doubleheader with the Pittsburgh Pirates when Ed Mosler hosted me along with Football Giants' stars Frank Gifford and Charlie Connerly. It was the last weekend baseball game played in the historic Polo Grounds.

Before the game Bob Prince, the broadcast voice of the Pirates, was walking around the field and when he saw us, came over to talk. I knew him when I was at West Virginia University when he broadcast Pittsburgh's football games. He asked me to bring Frank to the press box for an interview between the two games and I was pleasantly surprised when he asked me to stay and be on air with him for the next 10 minutes.

The Giants said goodbye to New York the next day after 75 seasons and lost to Pittsburgh 9-1 before 11,606 fans. Two years later I "followed" the Giants to San Francisco.

Chapter 16

Some Of My Favorite Places

During my life I have been fortunate to have lived in and traveled to many places. I have called home Charleston and Morgantown, West Virginia; Norfolk and Virginia Beach, Virginia; Toledo, Ohio; San Francisco; Los Angeles; New York City; Washington, D.C.; Bryan/College Station, Texas; Philadelphia; Green Valley, Arizona; West Palm Beach, Florida; and now Seattle. I have traveled in 47 states and missed only Montana, and North and South Dakota. I consider myself very lucky to have seen so many parts of our country and the world, have so many good friends and to have met many interesting people.

I've been to and seen the Great Wall of China; the Terra Cotta Warriors; the great pyramids of Ghiza; the Sphinx; Niagara Falls; Grand Canyon; been to the top of the Empire State Building and the Washington Monument; Arc de Triomphe; Eiffel Tower; Gibraltar; the Parthenon on the Acropolis; Rome's Colosseum; Rio's Sugarloaf Mountain and Christ the Redeemer; and scores of other wonderful places.

One Of My Favorite Cities

Washington, D.C. has always been one of my favorite cities even when Marion Barry was the mayor. My first trip was with a junior high school class. Later I attended meetings there when in high school. For years taxis charged by zones and if I went to a Washington Senators baseball game we would get off two blocks before Griffith Stadium to save having to pay for another zone. In the 1960s and 1970s I was a frequent visitor on business and then lived there for six years in the 1980s. My two-story condo was on the top floor of a mixed-used building, had a wood-burning fireplace and a balcony view sweeping from Rock Creek Park to DuPont Circle.

The 4th of July is always special in Washington. My neighbors and I would go to our building's roof which provided a great view for the fireworks. Someone would always have a TV set tuned to the program on The Mall and playing patriotic music.

I could go out my front door and walk two blocks to Georgetown on M Street and have a choice of outstanding restaurants. I loved riding my bike along the towpath of the C&O Canal by the Potomac River; through Rock Creek Park to the zoo; to spend time at the Lincoln and Jefferson Memorials; and along the Mall and around the Capitol. Sometimes I would drive to Arlington to meet my friend John Mosher and we would ride our bikes through Old Town in Alexandria and halfway to Mount Vernon on a path along the Potomac.

I loved walking through the Capitol and under the magnificent rotunda both as a tourist and when I had business with members of Congress. This freedom of access no longer exists. When I worked at the Department of Labor I enjoyed playing softball for our Labor Pains team in the Bush League on the Ellipse by the Washington Monument. Almost all of the great museums were free and I often visited the Smithsonian and Hirshorn museums and the latter's sculpture garden. Union station is one one of the classic railroad stations in the country. Until the city fathers let it fall into nearly total disrepair, the Metro was one of the best transit systems in the U.S., clean, safe and graffiti-free. When I shopped at the Safeway in Georgetown I never knew who I might meet at the produce or meat-fish sections.

There has always been fine dining in Washington. Hot Shoppes and White Castle accommodated eating on a budget. Unfortunately, many popular restaurants have long closed their kitchens: Duke Ziebert's, Dominique's, Sans Souci, Rive Gauche, McPherson Grill, Le Lion d'Or, and Jean-Pierre. My current list of favorites includes La Chaumiere, 1789, Filomena Ristorante, Old Ebbitt Grill, The George Town Club, Clyde's of Georgetown, The Palm, and on Capitol Hill, The Monocle.

New York, New York

New York indeed is a wonderful town. I always loved visiting the city but the one year I lived there was enough for me to not want to be a full-time resident. I saw my first Broadway play, *Oklahoma*, at the St. James Theatre in 1946 with a $3.00 balcony seat. Theatre ticket prices were very affordable then and I found some old stubs as low as $1.50 for an orchestra seat. Prices increased a decade later and without paying scalper's prices you had to know someone to get tickets to see sold out shows and especially Mary Martin in *The Sound of Music* and Julie Andrews in *My Fair Lady*. There were no half-price tickets in Times Square in those days. When I was on active military duty I often got free tickets from the USO to many shows.

I spent many hours in two of the world's classic railroad stations: Penn Station and Grand Central Station. It was a shame Penn Station was destroyed for the new Madison Square Garden and that architects would not preserve its historic beauty.

The movie theaters once had stage shows with name bands and artists who performed between movies. Radio City Music Hall featured the Rockettes and Dick Liebert at the organ. I saw a young Frank Sinatra sing first at the Paramount, a decade later at the Copacabana, and his finale in Atlantic City in 1980 with Dean Martin and Sammy Davis, Jr. I enjoy watching the ice skaters and walking around the giant Christmas tree at Rockefeller Center during the holidays. A cruise then was a trip on the Staten Island ferry or the Circle Line cruise around Manhattan.

Dining on a budget was at the Horn and Hardart Automat, Schrafft's or Nedick's. During college, Greenwich Village with Eddie Condon's and Nick's were my places for jazz and Julius' and Louie's for a beer. Joe King's German-American Rathskeller and Luchow's also were affordable places. By the 1960s I had upgraded to my college friend Norman Moomjian's Copain, Toots Shor's, 21, Sardi's, Mamma Leone's, P.J. Clarke's, Carnegie Deli, Grand Central Oyster Bar, McSorley's Old Ale House and Chumley's, the historic pub and former speakeasy in the Village. And in its heyday in the 1970s, Studio 54. I still enjoy shopping at Zabar's and for cheese at Alleva's in Little Italy. Today Daniel and Café Boulud are at the top of my dining list.

Over the years I have stayed at a score of hotels including the Plaza, Carlyle, St. Regis, St. Moritz, Elysée, Grand Hyatt, Essex House, J.W. Marriott, Pierre and Warwick depending where and with whom I had business. My most frequent stays were at the New York Hilton, Waldorf Astoria and Marriott East Side. The Waldorf gave members of the U.S. Olympic Committee a discount and room upgrades when Hilton was a sponsor. It and the Marriott East Side are located a couple of blocks from the 51st Street Lexington Avenue subway station which made it convenient when I had business downtown. The Hilton on Avenue of the Americas between 49th and 50th Streets was convenient when I had business in the Rockefeller Center area. For luxury and impeccable service I chose the Plaza Athénée, much like its "twin" in Paris. A favorite until it converted to apartments was the Beekman Tower, a classic Art Deco hotel a block from the United Nations at the corner of 1st Avenue and 49th Street next to tony Sutton Place. Its Top of the Tower lounge on the 26th floor had a fantastic view of the skyline and was one of the most romantic places in the city.

I loved going to the 1942 New York World's Fair, Frank Buck's Jungleland on Long Island, Jones Beach, and to the top of the Empire State Building. I have rain checks from baseball games of the Yankees in Yankee Stadium, the Giants in the Polo Grounds, and the Brooklyn Dodgers in Ebbets Field with prices ranging from

$1.25 for grandstand seats to $3.00 in 1949 for a lower stand box seat. Then you could get a bag of peanuts for a nickel, a hot dog for a dime and a beer for no more than a quarter. You could take a family to a game and day at the ballpark for less than the cost of a single ticket today.

I spent hours in Madison Square Garden when it was on 8th Avenue between 49th and 50th Streets to see rodeos, ice shows, the circus, basketball and hockey games. During the 1957-58 season, when both colleges and professional teams played double headers and when I was on active duty at West Point I didn't miss one game. Lester Scott, who ran press operations for the Garden, took good care of me. When a newspaper needed coverage he would give me the assignment. Other times I provided scouting reports on New York college teams for their opponents to supplement my $63 a month military pay.

Dim Sum And Den Some

When I lived in New York or was there on business I always met my friend John Lynch on Saturday for dim sum brunch in Chinatown. I would stay in mid-town and take the subway to Canal Street and walk along the various stores and shops to Mott Street where we met at the Oriental Pearl. Often we would be the only Caucasians dining in the restaurant.

After feasting on a variety of dishes we walked to Little Italy and sometimes stopped for an espresso. We continued through SoHo and on to the West Village and an Italian bakery. John knew the best and always wanted his cannoli filled fresh so the pastry never got soggy. We finished in Washington Square where he lived and many times I continued walking up Fifth Avenue to my mid-town hotel.

South Of The Border, Down Mexico Way

I spent considerable time in Mexico City. The traffic is horrendous, the air quality terrible, and there are always problems getting to and from the airport to downtown. During the mid-1970s we sought to establish an ICPR office there so I was a frequent visitor. I stayed at the Maria Isabel on Paseo de Reforma by the El Angel monument. Being in the heart of the Zona Rosa it was a short walk to shop at Publico Mercado and have lunch at Fonda el Refugio or dinner at Anderson's-Reforma. My favorite restaurant was the world renowned San Angel Inn, especially for Sunday brunch. Other dining favorites were Fonda del Recuerdo, Anderson's-Chapultepec, and Meson Caballo del Bayo.

On every trip I tried to find time to visit the Museo Nacional de Antropologío, one of the world's great museums. I also spent time in the Zócalo, Palacio de Bellas Artes and driving through Bosque de Chapultepec, the largest urban park in Latin America. I liked to walk through Catedral Metropolitana, the largest cathedral in Latin America. My other favorite Mexican cities include Cuernavaca with its five-star Las Mañanitas restaurant; San Miguel de Allende; Merida; Tepoztlán, surrounded by massive antennae where some residents claim to have met with aliens; Alamos; Guadalajara; Guanajuato; Puerto Vallarta; Cabo San Lucas; the preserved Mayan ruins and pyramids of Chichen Itza, Tulum, Uxmal, and Tikal; and the fabulous El Chepe train ride from Chihuahua to Los Mochis through Copper Canyon and 87 tunnels and over 36 bridges.

Other Wonderful Memories

My first car was a six-year-old 1946 black two-door Ford. My first new car, a 1954 four-door Chevrolet Bel Air. The Steel Pier in Atlantic City in the 1950s and the diving horses. College Spring break in Daytona Beach. Taking a college date to Frank Dailey's Meadowbrook on the Newark-Pompton Turnpike in Cedar Grove, N.J. to dance and hear one of the era's great big bands. Disneyland. Walt Disney World. Big Sur. Niagara Falls. Yosemite. Arizona's Grand Canyon and Chirichua National Park, once home to Indian warriors Geronimo and Cochise. Bar Harbor and Acadia National Park. Sedona and Oak Creek Canyon. Standing on the running board of a San Francisco cable car climbing California Street. Monticello. Mt. Vernon.

Egypt – The Sphinx and the Great Pyramids of Giza; Karnak; Luxor; Valley of the Kings; Tomb of Tut-ankh-Amun; Temple of Queen Hatshepsut; Cairo Egyptian Museum. Malta – Valletta; the Neolithic Temples of Tarxien, and Ġgantija on Gozo, built 3800-2200 B.C., older than the pyramids; Mdina; Blue Grotto; watchtowers of the Knights of St. John.

Greece – Athens. The Parthenon on the Acropolis; Pantheon; National Historical Museum; Constitution Square; Dionysus Theater; Temple of Olympian Zeus; Panathinaiko Stadium where the 1896 Olympic Games were held. The Corinth Canal that separates the Peloponnese peninsula from the Greek mainland. The 13th-14th Century B.C. ruins of Mycenae and the Tomb of Agamemnon. The seaport town of Nafplio and its Palmidi Castle.

St. Petersburg, Russia - The Hermitage; Catherine's Palace; Peterhof fountains; St. Isaac's Cathedral; The Alexander Column; Mariinsky Theatre; Church of the Spilled Blood; art and crystal chandeliers in the subways; a boat ride through the canals. Reykjavik, Iceland - Hallgrimskirkja church; Blue Lagoon; The Pearl. Helsinki - Tuomiokirkko Cathedral; Senate Square; Temppelinkio, the Rock Church.

More History – France, Italy And Belgium

Rome - The Colosseum; The Forum; Pantheon; Trevi Fountain; Borghese Gallery; Spanish Steps; Circus Maximus; Via Condotti; Vatican City, St. Peter's Basilica, St. Peter's Square, and the Sistine Chapel. Venice - St. Mark's Square; Harry's Bar; Rialto Bridge; Bridge of Sighs; Doge's Palace. Milan - La Scala opera house; 14th Century Gothic cathedral Il Duomo; and connecting the two, Galleria Vittorio Emanuele II, one of the world's first shopping malls; Milano Centrale railroad station. Matera and its Sassi caves; Ostuni. Alberobello and the 16th Century truilli dwellings with conical roofs. Mt. Vesuvius. Pompeii. Positano and the Amalfi Coast. Turin with its wide covered sidewalks, so you can walk anywhere without getting wet, and looking behind the preserved antique facades to see a new, modern building. Ladispoli - La Posta

Vecchia boutique hotel and former residence of J. Paul Getty. Porto Venere, gateway to Cinque Terra.

Paris - Arc de Triomphe; Eiffel Tower; Le Louvre; Notre Dame Cathédral; Centre Pompidou; Montmartre; Bois de Boulogne; Au Trou Gascon. Normandy - Mont-St.-Michel; The World War II Omaha and Utah beaches and cemetery; Sainte-Mère-Église. San Malo. Deauville. Nice. Cannes. Roger Vergé's Moulin de Mougins. Vallauris and the Picasso Madura Gallery. Eze and Château de la Chêvre d'Or. Saint-Jean-Cap-Ferrat. Driving through Bordeaux and its wine regions of Saint-Émilion, Médoc, Margaux, Saint-Julien, Paulliac and Pomerol and visiting world famous wineries.

Brussels - Grand Place; Royal Galleries of Saint-Hubert; Manneken Pis. Antwerp. Jumet and Marchienne au Pont, where my paternal grandparents were born. A boat ride in the canals of Brugge. Knokke-Heist. Spa. Liege. Brasschaat.

And More...

Dubai and its outrageous extravagance – Emirates Mall and its indoor ski slopes; riding in a Jeep over sand dunes; Burj Al Arab hotel; the souks. Casablanca. Oman. Shanghai - The Bund; Shanghai Museum. Beijing - Tiananmen Square; Birds Nest National Olympic Stadium; Forbidden City; Summer Palace. Chongqing, China's largest city with 32 million people. The Three Gorges Dam. Great Wall of China. The Ming Tombs. Xi'an - the 210 B.C. life-size terracotta warriors; city walls; the small and large Wild Goose Pagodas; Bell and Drum Towers.

London - Westminster Abbey; walking along The Thames; Tower of London; Piccadilly Circus; Buckingham Palace; Tower Bridge; Trafalgar Square; Joe Allen's Restaurant; theatres; fish and chip stands. Roman Baths in Bath. Stonehenge.

Bombay (Mumbai), India - Gateway to India; Taj Mahal Hotel; Ghandi's home. Phuket, Thailand. Burma (Myanmar) - Rangoon (Yangon), Shwedagon Pagoda; Bago, the ancient capital; Kyakhatwine Monastery; Shwemeawdaw Pagoda; the Buddhas at Kyeikpon. Hong Kong. Singapore. Tokyo.

Lisbon – the mall from Praça de Comércio on the River Tigus to Praça de Restauradores, the Elevador de Gloriá to the top of one of the city's seven hills; the Elevador de Santa Justa, an historic wrought-iron vertical street lift down to an area of superb restaurants; Castelo de São Jorge overlooking the city and a bridge that could double as San Francisco's Golden Gate. Sydney and its Opera House, bridge and harbor; The Rocks. Perth - black swans in the lake; nearby Freemantle, site of the 1987 America's Cup.

The Caribbean - St. Croix; St. Thomas; St. John; Tortola; Little Dix Bay; Sint Maarten; Saint-Martin; Guadeloupe; Martinique; Barbados; Trinidad & Tobago; Cap Juluca in Anguilla; Dominican Republic; Puerto Rico – San Juan and Old San Juan; Dorado Beach; Humacoa; Ponce; and the El Conquistador in Fajardo.

Copenhagen - Hop-On-Hop-Off Bus to get around; the Little Mermaid sculpture; Tivoli Gardens; Amalienborg Palace; and the freetown of Christiania settled by hippies in 1971. Stockholm - the cobblestone streets of Gamma Stan; the Old Town; Hop-On-Hop-Off Bus and Boat; Royal Palace; Vasa Museum; Parliament; Central Station; City Hall and the auditorium of the building where Nobel Prizes are awarded.

Vancouver, B.C. - Stanley Park; Granville Island; Gastown; Vancouver Lookout; Lion's Gate Bridge. Gibraltar - the Barbary apes; Lighthouse Point. Monaco - Grand Casino; Hôtel de Paris. Guernsey. Amsterdam - Van Gogh Museum; Rijksmuseum; the canals. Waterford, the oldest city in Ireland, founded by the Vikings in 914 A.D. and famous for its crystal most of which is now made in Slovenia, Germany, Hungary and Czech Republic. In an Irish pub watching Kilkenny and Tipperary play to a draw in the All-Ireland Senior National Hurling Championship Final, Ireland's equivalent to the U.S. Super Bowl. Dublin - the Spire; Harp Bridge; Trinity College and the Book of Kells; St. Patrick's Cathedral. Belfast - The Peace Walls; McHugh's Pub; Parliament.

Cape Cod and fresh lobster. Nantucket. Martha's Vineyard. The Canadian Maritime Provinces. Nova Scotia - Halifax; Peggy's Cove; Lunenberg; Cape Breton; the Evangeline Trail; Bay of

Fundy. Prince Edward Island - Charlottetown; Malpeque Bay. New Brunswick - Moncton; Hopewell Rocks; Campobello and the Franklin D. Roosevelt family home.

Chile - Santiago; Valparaiso; Viña del Mar; Puerto Montt; Punta Arenas. Ushuaia, Argentina, the southernmost city in the world. Montevideo, Uruguay. Buenos Aires, the Paris of South America. Rio de Janeiro - Sugarloaf; Ipanema Beach; Christ the Redeemer Statue; Copacabana Beach.

The train from Anchorage to Fairbanks, Alaska. Denali Park. Canoeing down the river from the Portage Glacier with fantastic scenery and wildlife. Catching a 42-pound king salmon on the Kenai Peninsula. Barcelona - Gaudi's La Sagrada Familia Basilica; Parc Güell; Parc Montjuïc; Els 4 Gats Restaurant where Picasso designed the menu cover; Montserrat.

Holland, Germany, Austria And Hungary

Until 2016 a Danube River boat trip had been on my bucket list for three decades. In 1983 I spent a week in Budapest judging a sports film festival and at the World Gymnastics Championships. After dinner several of us walked on the Promenade along the Danube between Chain Bridge and Parliament and we saw some 30 people elegantly dressed – women in evening gowns and men in black tie – on a small boat being served champagne by waiters in white tie and tails and violinists providing music. I knew then I wanted to take this trip.

The dress code has since changed but the service was exceptional on a Viking longboat for 15 days from Amsterdam to Budapest. We cruised through canals and locks on the Rhine, Main and Danube Rivers and through beautiful medieval towns with winding cobblestone streets and half-timbered houses, magnificent cathedrals and towering castles. Nuremberg was interesting and historic being the site of Hitler's many rallies and the trials of the Nazi war criminals. In Melk black-robed Benedictine monks stroll the halls of the 900-year-old abbey that dominates the hillside. Vienna was beautiful with its Belvedere, Habsburg and

Schönbrunn Palaces, giant Ferris wheel and much more. Budapest was a special treat the way the buildings on the Danube are illuminated at night. Viking served us tastes of all local foods, Bavarian beers, Rhine and Wachau Valley wines, and deserts that included apple strudel and Sacher-Torte. There were only 180 passengers on board and with open seating for all meals you became acquainted and friends with everyone.

Planes, Trains, Boats And Food

New Orleans is food, jazz and Mardi Gras; Galatoire's; Arnaud's; Brennan's; Commander's Palace; Oysters Rockefeller at Antoine's. A Cobb salad at the Hollywood Brown Derby the way Bob Cobb intended it to be made and served. A Singapore Sling at Raffles Hotel in Singapore. A Bellini with Carpaccio at Harry's Bar in Venice or an espresso in Caffé Florian on St. Mark's Square, opened in 1720 and the world's oldest café. Many of my favorite Los Angeles restaurants are now gone – Scandia, Cock 'n' Bull, La Famiglia, Ma Maison, Chasen's, Señor Pico, Jumpin' Frog Saloon among others. When Patrick Terrail opened Ma Maison in 1975 with Wolfgang Puck as his chef the restaurant had an unlisted telephone number. You had to know Patrick to get a dinner reservation.

My first flight - Capital Airlines from Charleston, West Virginia to Cincinnati in 1950. Riding the California Zephyr several times from San Francisco to Chicago in December in the early 1960s with fantastic scenery through the California Sierras and Colorado Rockies and being on time. Overnight on the 20th Century Limited from New York to Chicago. My first jet flight, an American Boeing 707, December 1959 from Chicago to San Francisco, all one class seating. Jet boat up the Snake River through Idaho's Hell's Canyon, the deepest gorge in North America. A paddlewheeler on the Columbia River following the route of Lewis and Clark. Cruising the Yangtze River. Transiting the Panama Canal. Cruising the Suez Canal. The Strait of Gibraltar. Sailing around Cape Horn off Tierra del Fuego on the Crystal Symphony with massive 45-foot waves and hurricane force 70-knot winds battering the ship.

Olympic stadiums in Athens, Barcelona, Beijing, Helsinki and of course the Los Angeles Coliseum. The Rose Bowl. The Washington Senators in Griffith Stadium. Granby High School winning the Virginia state high school basketball championship in 1950. West Virginia in 1955 winning the first of many Southern Conference basketball tournament championships. At the finish line for a race segment of the Giro di Italia in Turin, Italy. At all home games of 1971-72 Los Angeles Lakers winning 33 straight games. The 1970 playoff game against the New York Knicks when Jerry West made a 60-foot shot to tie the game as the buzzer sounded. Regrettably, the Knicks won in overtime.

It is especially enjoyable when you unexpectedly meet friends when traveling. On a cruise ship one day after leaving Valparaiso, Chile, I ran into Eddie and Betty Barrett, David and Susan Hardesty, and other friends who were part of a West Virginia University alumni travel group. For the next two weeks I became part of their group. One of our shore excursions was a fascinating visit to the Punta Tombo penguin rookery, a colony of more than one-and-one-half million Magellan penguins on the Patagonian coast of Argentina. It was a two-hour drive from our port of Puerto Madryn and the last 40 miles on a gravel road. It is a UNESCO World Heritage site and well worth the time and trip because penguins are all around you and it is possible to literally walk by their side along shore paths and their natural habitat.

Chapter 17

A New World

So much in the world has changed during my lifetime. It is definitely not the same anymore. The Taliban, Al Queada, ISIS and other terror groups and radicals have changed the way we travel. Security is everywhere. I remember when you could freely come and go in all of the buildings in Washington, D.C. You looked forward to airline travel and not the compliance required by Homeland Security.

It would take several books just to list all of the wonders and miracles I've experienced. I do not believe that all of the new electronic technology has necessarily made things better. The proliferation of social media is impacting behavior and not positively. With pads, pods, berries and the like there is less and less verbal communication. People walk around all thumbs into their devices, their ears plugged with buds, and oblivious to the world around them. I believe that some people actually believe it is correct to tweet or email a sympathy to someone who has lost a loved one. I wonder if they have ever seen, much less written, an informal card.

Few people say "hello" these days. Even fewer hold a door or elevator for you, much less thank you if you do so for them. Can you remember a luncheon or dinner when men stood up while a woman was being seated? Or opened a car door for a woman? We have a generation that doesn't have a clue that their actions are rude, inconsiderate, and insulting and violate every basic tenet of good old fashioned common courtesy.

The Dress Code

Much has changed in the public relations and advertising professions since I started in the business. My first wardrobe was like that of Don Draper of the popular television series *Mad Men*. I had two or three hats I wore to complement a suit, tie and white shirt. You wouldn't think of wearing a blue blazer for a business meeting. People wore a suit and tie when traveling on an airplane and always when dining at a restaurant. When I was in college I remember men had to wear a jacket to even ride in the elevator at some New York hotels.

By the 1970s, business dress in many businesses in Los Angeles was casual – even more casual than today's business casual. Exceptions were made depending on dinner reservations. For years a coat and tie was required at a number of leading restaurants including New York's 21 and Ernie's in San Francisco. Another exception was Hollywood where "informal" meant black tie and "formal" meant white tie and tails. Because of many client functions I wore black tie more often than even a jacket and tie.

Wall Street had its own dress code. When I had my own consulting practice, I went through a period of near shoulder-length hair, double knits, boots and expensive kid-glove leather jackets. Once I walked into the lobby at Bache & Company and the male receptionist, without looking up, pointed to the door and said officiously, "All deliveries are at the rear." I placed my Gucci briefcase on his desk, pulled out my business card and said, "John Roosevelt is expecting me." Roosevelt, the youngest child of Franklin Delano Roosevelt, was vice president of Bache and I was working with him on a financial project for a client. The male receptionist – almost all were men on Wall Street during this period – stammered, stuttered and may have fouled himself before he announced me to Roosevelt's secretary.

In the 1980s and 1990s dress varied depending on where I was working. For sports marketing clients and meetings a blue blazer, grey slacks and tie was the preferred dress. In Washington, D.C. for business it meant a dark, pin-striped suit and tie that we referred to as the "uniform." I remember one August month when the temperature exceeded 100 degrees 10 days in a row with the humidity nearly 100 percent. You were drenched in perspiration after walking just one or two blocks.

When "business casual" became popular I was vice president and public relations counsel to Jeff Prosser who owned Innovative Communication Corporation. Our headquarters were in Christiansted, St. Croix, U.S. Virgin Islands, and our management offices in West Palm Beach. Jeff's dress code was suit and tie – not even a blazer and tie. This is what I wore whenever I was on business in the U.S. and British Virgin Islands, Guadeloupe, Martinique, Sint Maarten, Saint-Martin, Belize, Trinidad & Tobago, Barbados or any Caribbean island. This was my last professional job and I virtually came full circle in apparel.

Now that I live in Seattle, about the only time I wear a suit and tie is for church or a memorial service. Seldom do I even need a blazer with or without a tie. I do not know of a local restaurant that requires a jacket, much less a tie. Today in the Pacific Northwest it is not unusual to see the serving staff dressed better than the diners, some of whom wear shorts, baseball caps and flip flops. Many private clubs in the East still require a jacket in dining rooms.

The Change In Communicating

Electronic technology, the Internet, Bing, Google and Wikipedia have made it so much easier to do research. I remember when we needed to find answers and research projects we spent hours in the library searching through books and publications. Today a few clicks will get answers but not always correct ones. And too few people double check to be sure the information they use is correct. The worst are inexperienced journalists too eager to be first with a story.

New technology has completely changed the way we communicate and increased the amount of information that we can quickly disseminate, much less assimilate. I started writing with a Remington portable manual typewriter when I was in junior high school and taught myself how to type. When typing was part of a battery of U.S. Army induction tests I typed 96 words a minute on a manual. I was thrilled when I owned my first IBM Correcting Selectric electric typewriter and could exceed 120 words a minute. In fact, I have one that I use at times.

The computer with word processing and the Internet took us into a new age. When I authored my first book in 1976 it was no easy task making changes. When I needed to make a change or insert a paragraph on say page three of a 25-page chapter, I had to retype all of the pages. There was no such thing as cut-and-paste. If you needed multiple copies you had to use carbon paper and were always careful not to make a typing error that would need to be corrected. The copy machine eliminated the need for carbon paper. I preferred writing with Word Perfect, a word processing program comparable to Microsoft Word, and many of my writer and lawyer friends agree. Unfortunately, few people use it today making it difficult to communicate.

We went from rotary dial to push button telephones to cell phones, Blackberries, iPhones, smart phones, iPods and pads. There was no Facebook, Linked-in or Twitter. Sometimes I believe we are in an era of over information and not only getting more than we want, but more than we need. This may impact on productivity.

The Days Of Radio

When I was growing up there was no television. There was only radio. Most programs were 15 minutes in length and challenged the mind and imagination in ways television does not. As you listened to your favorite programs you had to conceive how, where and what was happening as the story unfolded. My grandmother loved to listen to the Metropolitan Opera from New York on Saturday mornings and she had her favorite afternoon soap operas that included *Portia Faces Life* and *Guiding Light*. Several became popular daytime television series.

Some of my favorite radio programs included *Lone Ranger, Inner Sanctum, Fibber McGee & Molly, Amos 'n' Andy, The Great Gildersleeve, Abbott & Costello, Jack Benny, Your Hit Parade, The Shadow, Red Skelton, Major Bowes Amateur Hour, Edgar Bergen & Charlie McCarthy, Duffy's Tavern, The Green Hornet,* and *Lum and Abner*. I also listened to the Cincinnati Reds baseball games with my step-grandfather, Pop Secrest.

Television did not become readily available for most families until the 1950s. The most popular network news program was John Cameron Swayze's 15-minute-long *Camel News Caravan* on NBC. In 1956, a week after CBS launched its network news featuring Walter Cronkite, this was replaced with an expanded half-hour news program anchored by Chet Huntley and David Brinkley. Local news has increased and now with so many cable networks viewers can see news 24 hours a day. However, the trust factor of the American public in what they are seeing and hearing has never been the same since Huntley, Brinkley, Cronkite and Edward R. Murrow retired.

The *Today Show* started in 1952 with founding host Dave Garroway. Most mornings he worked alone but sometimes would be joined by his "co-host" J. Fred Muggs, a chimpanzee. The show today must have at least a half dozen regulars doing the same thing he did. Bill Stern, one of the greatest sports announcers of all time, worked alone. Watching a game today you have a cadre of announcers telling you everything you are seeing on television and repeating what you've seen and already know.

Writing And Style Are Lost

We have people in the media and public relations who cannot write and do not double check their facts. News staffs have been slashed and what few investigative reporters there are do not take the time to research and develop stories as they once did. This, combined with pressure to be the first to break a news story, has led to misleading and wrong information being broadcast.

At ICPR one of our account executives, Jay Berman, gave all new applicants a writing test. He also taught courses in the Annenberg School for Journalism and Communication at the University of Southern California. He was thorough and detailed and even in the 1970s few college graduates could pass his test. One friend said with the exception of a B grade in one of Jay's classes she had straight A's at USC.

I doubt if many of the professors and instructors responsible for educating journalism and public relations majors today could pass his basic writing test. I have always used the Associated Press Stylebook as a guide for writing style, abbreviation, capitalization, and punctuation. I would require this as one of the first "textbooks" for a student majoring in journalism or public relations. It would be a life-long tool for them. I question how many professors even have a copy in their personal library.

The AP Stylebook is a 400-plus page wealth of information that I have recommended as a library and writing tool for lawyers and others in business. For example, too many young journalists and PR practitioners wrongfully use the state abbreviations of the U.S. Postal Service with AZ instead of the Stylebook guidelines Ariz., CA and not Calif., WV and not West Virginia. There are eight states that are never abbreviated: Alaska, Hawai'i, Idaho, Iowa, Maine, Ohio, Texas and Utah.

Television announcers should know better when they talk about a *new* world record instead of a world record period. Every four years during Olympic broadcasts this is repeated time and again when a record is broken and the sportscaster will call it a *new* world record instead of just a record. Or we hear about the *first* annual when it isn't annual until the second time.

Another common mistake of television announcers is mispronouncing the name of the French Riviera resort of Cannes. You would think a network news anchor would know better but too often I've heard Cannes pronounced as Caen, an important city in Normandy some 705 miles away. Cannes is simply pronounced "can" like a tin can, while Caen is "kawhn" to rhyme with lawn. Someday I hope an airline representative or travel agent sends one of these people to Caen when they want to go to Cannes.

Political Correctness

Today if someone feels offended for virtually any reason this can lead to a protest or demonstration. Colleges seem to be under the greatest pressure for change and many have been very quick to respond to any protest. College professors have come under fire for recommended reading or a topic in a lecture that a student found offensive.

Harvard Law School changed its logo because it was modeled on the family crest of an 18th century slaveholder. Students at Princeton demanded all images of Woodrow Wilson be removed because they consider him a racist. Amherst College no longer has any references to Lord Jeffrey Amherst, the Colonial-era military commander after whom the town and college are named, because he gave smallpox-infected blankets to Native Americans. The college removed the Lord Jeffrey name from its campus hotel and Lord Jeffs is no longer the mascot name. Alumni are divided over the issue. The trustees made no mention of changing the name of the college or the town.

Students at the University of Cape Town in South Africa had a campus statue of Cecil Rhodes removed and have called for Oxford to do the same where he endowed scholarships. Rhodes was a British businessman, mining magnate and Prime Minister of the Cape Colony. The student protestors call him the "Hitler of southern Africa." Alumni at Oxford's Oriel College threatened to withdraw their financial support unless they rejected the students' demands.

For years Alaska Airlines has had the face of an Eskimo on the tail of all of its planes. But when it introduced a new and refreshed brand it had the line "Meet our Eskimo" which offended the Alaska Native community. Alaska CEO Brad Tilden immediately apologized, took full responsibility and the airline replaced the word "our" with "the" to read "Meet the Eskimo." I believe Alaska's public relations and customer service programs are the best in the industry.

In the mid-2000s the National Collegiate Athletic Association ordered its member colleges to change mascots and nicknames if any could be considered "hostile and offensive" to Native Americans. Central Michigan, Florida State, Mississippi College and Utah all fought back and did not change. The Washington Redskins professional football team has been under pressure by Congress and many organizations to change its name.

Soon companies, organizations and institutions are going to have to make decisions as to what degree changes will be made to accommodate people who are offended for any reason and want the solution to be rewriting history. ISIS plundered and destroyed nearly 30 historic buildings and left the ancient city of Palmyra in Syria in ruins. Islamic militants consider the looting and destruction of such centuries old historic and religious buildings and artifacts a form of cultural cleansing and sell some of the valuable artifacts to finance their activities. An example of extreme religious intolerance of the Taliban was the 2001 destruction of the Buddhas of Bamiyan, two 6th Century statues carved in the side of a cliff. Standing nearly 175 feet and 125 feet tall, the monuments were the largest examples of standing Buddha carvings in the world.

I believe what has happened in the past is done and can't be changed. I believe efforts today should focus on the future and to remember the advice of philosopher George Santayana: "Those who do not remember the past are condemned to repeat it."

Money Wins Elections

Thanks to the John Roberts led Supreme Court we are a nation where the wealthiest can spend whatever amount of money they want to buy and elect their chosen representatives and to determine results on issues. Political Action Committees and Super PAC's dominate elections. Critics say the system has become so corrupt that is is undermining democracy. Billions of dollars are wasted that could be used in so many ways to benefit society. I would love to see us adopt the way the British do it with the entire campaign over in a matter of months and with spending limits.

In 2010 when the Supreme Court voted 5-4 along party lines in the Citizens United v. FEC case it overturned sections of the McCain-Feingold Campaign Reform Act of 2002 and loosened restrictions on spending by corporations, unions and advocacy groups. PACs and Super Pacs now can do just about anything a campaign or political party can do including voter registration efforts, sending direct-mail pieces or making automated telephone calls, but don't have the same financial limits and donor disclosure requirements that candidates' campaigns do. Subsequent rulings by the Federal Election Commission have given groups the ability to raise and spend unlimited amounts of money on political issues.

John Cox, a wealthy Republican entrepreneur and attorney from San Diego, committed $1 million for paid canvassers to get a ballot initiative that would require members of the state legislature to wear stickers or badges of the names of their top 10 campaign contributors on their suits and dresses. Appropriately named the "Name All Sponsors California Accountability Reform" initiative, or short for NASCAR where the race drivers and cars are plastered with logo decals.

Cox even had 121 life-size cutouts of legislators and Governor Jerry Brown set up outside the capitol building decorated with logos including AT&T, Occidental Petroleum, Walmart, Eli Lilly, Chevron and Altria tobacco. His ballot measure also would require disclosure statements of donors on political advertisements.[33]

Should the initiative pass, First Amendment experts are divided on whether it could survive a lawsuit. "It essentially forces officeholders to act as state billboards whenever they are acting in their official capacity," says a skeptical Timothy Zick, a law professor at the College of William & Mary. "This a case of compulsory

---

33 Valerie Richardson, *The Washington Times*; November 26, 2015; Steven Nelson, *US News*, December 30, 2015; and Joseph Weber, FoxNews.com, April 6, 2016.

speech and not a tailored way to address fraud and transparency."[34]

Cox is certainly making a point to the voting public that all too often elected officials act more on behalf of the companies, organizations and lobbyists who financed their campaigns than the voters who elected them.

---

[34] Nelson, *op.cit.*; Robert Baldwin III, *Huffington Post*, February 10, 2016.

Epilogue

I thank God every day for the wonderful life I have lived and for my two absolutely wonderful children and their families, my parents, grand parents, step-father and family. I am thankful for the many friends I have and those who have passed. I am thankful for my good health, especially my mind, and God having given me the talent to write.

I am so proud of my daughter and son and how successful they have been in their chosen careers. Both got an early start in business. Deborah became the first female carrier for the *Santa Monica Evening News* and within several months was named "Carrier of the Month." Bruce followed her a year later. Their success in business has continued.

I thank God for the wonderful life given me; for being given the ability to take words and tell stories; the successes I've had professionally in diverse careers; and all of my wonderful experiences. I know at times there has been a guardian angel protecting and looking after me.

I have worked for and with many terrific people. I have been fortunate to have been guided and inspired by several wise mentors. I am thrilled that in several jobs I have been able to leave significant footprints. The campaign I launched in 1970 to allow pension fund investments in residential mortgage securities helped create the secondary mortgage market and stabilize housing production. I am proud I was a part of the U.S. Department of Labor team that brought to life *The Glass Ceiling Initiative* but disappointed that even after 25 years there still is so much gender, race and income inequality. And while it was not adopted agency-wide by the Environmental Protection Agency and other federal departments and agencies as originally planned, the use of 100% recycled paper with 100% post-consumer fiber is still policy in the EPA's Mid-Atlantic States region.

Title IX, which became law in 1972, demanded equal opportunity for women to participate in any education program or activity where the institution receives federal funding. I do not believe the federal government has ever sanctioned a college or university for not being in compliance. Public employees in enforcement divisions who do not enforce should have their jobs eliminated. I regret that the presidents and chancellors at so many colleges and universities never accepted responsibility or controlled the growth of football. An NFL team has 55 players but college teams have 125 with 85 scholarships. Coaches with multimillion dollar salaries are often the highest paid public employee in the state. A virtual unlimited flow of money is corrupting college sports the way it is our political system.

I have always been a strong supporter of equal treatment and opportunities for all. I do not believe that rewriting history just to be politically correct is the answer. We can't change and should not try to rewrite history, but be politically correct by being positive, not with rhetoric, but with actions as we move ahead.

Unlike our founding fathers, we now have political parties so polarized and partisan that they refuse to work together for the benefit of the American public. More politicians are driven by individual ideologies than the wishes of the voters who elected them to office. This has become so obvious with the way our presidential candidates are chosen in primaries and caucuses. When super delegates disregard the wishes of their constituents I feel my vote is disenfranchised. For decades Congress has talked about eliminating the Electoral College and using a popular vote in presidential elections. There is no stronger case than looking back to 2000 when Al Gore lost to George W. Bush even though he had 543,895 more votes. Let the people decide who they want.

I believe that if Congress refuses to vote on any bill of significant importance to the American public, or our Supreme Court is locked and cannot decide on a case, then the American public should decide. Place the issue or question on a nationwide ballot and have the result decided by the popular majority of all voters. I believe this expense should be borne by Congress by reducing their salaries, pensions and most of all, expenses for staff and travel. In recent years we have had do-nothing Congresses and they should be compensated based on performance and their salaries docked for absences.

We live in a society driven by waste and obsolescence. New football and baseball stadiums and basketball and ice hockey arenas are being built at tremendous taxpayer expense across the country to replace some not even 25 years old and in some instances where the bonded indebtedness has not even been retired. Politicians don't look at two of the nation's very best and oldest – the Rose Bowl and the Los Angeles Coliseum or even Boston's Fenway Park and Chicago's Wrigley Field. If a for-profit professional team makes unreasonable demands politicians should tell them to build their own facilities as a handful of other team owners have done.

I learned that sometimes being ahead of the curve is not always profitable. Some companies and organizations are just not ready to accept new ideas and concepts. When a concept becomes a trend it always is nice to take credit when and where credit is due for being the pioneer even though the competition may end up taking some or much of the profit. At ICPR we were 10 years ahead of the curve in the 1970s when we established the first Hispanic marketing division and the first full-service international sports marketing division in any advertising or public relations agency in the country. Those agencies that followed a decade later reaped the profits.

Our planet's environment is a disaster. The U.S. alone cannot reverse the damage that has been and is being done. I believe by the end of this century there will be totally new beachfronts in many parts of the world and some villages, towns and islands will no longer exist.

Too many in society today are rude and simply never learned the basics of common courtesy. It seems to get worse every year because of all of the technological advancements and a proliferation of social media and electronic devices. Words missing from many vocabularies are *please, thank you, you're welcome, excuse me,* and *I'm sorry.*

Some companies send you insulting do-not-reply emails and force you to go on line and take several steps to respond to one of their emails. Others have machines that play 20 questions with you when you want to speak to a live person even for the simplest of issues. You then hope your call is not outsourced to someone in a foreign country and the person you talk with has little command of the English language.

The worst are companies who have their employees lie and say "I work in the office of the president" when they are in an office hundreds or thousands of miles away and will never meet the president. When asked, some cannot even tell you the name of their president! They should just tell the truth and say they work in an area of customer service and have been asked to respond.

One of my major pet peeves is someone who does not know how rude it is to not return a phone call or respond to a letter, email or fax. All of the electronic technology has made it is easier now to do so than ever before. If only federal, state and local government employees would read and follow the Government Customer Service Improvement Act but most do not know that it exists.

I learned early in life from my parents, grand parents and step father to give back. Everyone can give back and it does not always have to be financially. I've been proud to mentor young professionals and recent graduates. Regardless of our level of experience there are others who can always use our advice. I've supported my alma mater financially and by being available to help with events and projects. Whenever asked, I've arranged my business schedule and returned to William & Mary at my expense. I've also supported West Virginia University, my church and other charities and non-profit organizations. I gave countless hours as a volunteer helping

Los Angeles become the host for the 1984 Olympic Games and then for the Los Angeles Olympic Organizing Committee and the U.S. Olympic Committee. I paid my expenses and volunteered for Global Volunteers to teach conversational English to high school and college students in Ostuni, Italy; Xi'an, China; and Dolores Hidalgo, Mexico.

Giving back is one of the easiest and most rewarding things a person can do.

Growing up I spent vacation time with my great aunt, Erna Nichols, at her home and farm in Jumpin' Branch, West Virginia. When I would get too restless and running around she would always say to me, "Now just sit down and be right easy." As I end this book, I'm going to do just that – sit down and be right easy.

Appendix

Rene A. Henry Professional Career
Chronological Employment

January 1953-June 1954 – Sports Information Director, The College of William & Mary, Williamsburg, Virginia, while still a full-time student.

June 1954-June 1956 – Sports Information Director, West Virginia University, Morgantown, West Virginia.

June-September 1956 – Account Executive, Flournoy & Gibbs, public relations, Toledo, Ohio.

October 1956-August 1958 – U.S. Army, Private First Class, assigned to the athletic department of the U.S. Military Academy at West Point, N.Y. Later served as First Lieutenant, U.S. Army Reserve-Armor until March 1965.

September 1958-September 1958 – Account Executive, Flournoy & Gibbs, public relations, Toledo, Ohio.

1958-1967 – Account Executive and then Publicity Director, Lennen & Newell, advertising, San Francisco, California.

1967-1970 – Vice President and Director of the Los Angeles Office, Daniel J. Edelman, public relations, Los Angeles, California.

1970-1974 – Chairman, President and CEO, Rene A. Henry, Inc., public relations, Los Angeles.

1974-1975 – Partner, Allan, Ingersoll, Segal & Henry, public relations, Beverly Hills, California.

1975-1980 – Co-Founder and Partner, ICPR, public relations, Los Angeles, California.

1980-1984 – President, Rene A. Henry Co., public relations, Los Angeles, California.

1985-1986 – President, Rene A. Henry Co., public relations, New York, N.Y.

1986-1988 – President and CEO, National Institute of Building Sciences, Washington, D.C.

1988 – Volunteer Campaign Director for Celebrities, George Bush for President and Bush/Quayle '88 presidential campaigns.

1989-1991 – Federal service in Washington, D.C. as Assistant to the Administrator, Farmers Home Administration, U.S. Department of Agriculture; Designate Assistant Administrator, U.S. Agency for International Development; and Assistant to the Director, Office of Federal Contract Compliance Programs, U.S. Department of Labor.

1991-1996 – Executive Director of University Relations and Member of the President's Executive Cabinet, Texas A&M University, College Station, Texas.

1996-2001 – Director of Communications and Government Relations, Mid-Atlantic States Region, U.S. Environmental Protection Agency, Philadelphia, Pennsylvania.

2001-2003 – Retired and Principal of Gollywobbler Productions, Green Valley, Arizona.

2003-2006 – Vice President of Public Relations and later Counselor to the Chairman, President and CEO, Innovative Communication Corporation, Christiansted, St. Croix, U.S. Virgin Islands and West Palm Beach, Florida.

2006-Current – Retired and Principal of Gollywobbler Productions, Seattle, Washington.

Education

The College of William & Mary, Williamsburg, Virginia, A.B., economics, June 1954.

West Virginia University, Morgantown, West Virginia. graduate work, marketing, 1954-1956.

Harvard University Law School, Cambridge, Massachusetts, executive management certificate course, conflict resolution, 1997.

Georgetown University Law School, Washington, D.C., executive management certificate course, liability of the federal employee, 1999.

Granby High School, Norfolk, Virginia, January 1951

Honors and Awards

- Awarded *The Alumni Medallion*, the highest honor the William & Mary Alumni Association bestows on a graduate of W&M, February 2011. Awarded the *Alumni Service Award* in 2004.
- Inducted into the Granby High School (Norfolk, Virginia) *Hall of Fame,* 2001.
- Inducted into the College of Fellows, Public Relations Society of America, 1994. Chair of the College in 2001. Recipient of the Paul Lund Award for Public Service, 2005.
- Joint Resolution from the Los Angeles City Council and Los Angeles County Board of Supervisors in recognition of outstanding leadership in bringing the 1984 Olympic Games to Los Angeles, June 29, 1984, the first joint City/County resolution ever issued.
- Clarion Award for Human Rights, 1981 (Women In Communication).
- *Distinguished Citizen Award* (Los Angeles Chapter/Public Relations Society of America), 1984

- Invested as a Knight of Grace in the Order of St. John of Jerusalem, Knights Hospitaller, May 2003. Promoted to Knight of Honour in November 2006. The Order of St. John is the oldest continuous order of chivalry in the world and the third oldest in Christianity.
- Three PRSA Silver Anvils (highest honor given in public relations)
- Six *PRisms Awards* (Los Angeles chapter of the Public Relations Society of America) and five *PRo Awards* (Los Angeles Publicity Club)
- Three CEBA Awards for Communications Excellence to Black Audiences (World Institute of Black Communications)
- "Best In Texas" *Silver Spurs* (Public Relations Society of Texas).
- San Francisco's *Public Relations Man of the Year* (San Francisco Bay Area Publicity Club), 1963
- One silver and two bronze medals from WorldFest Houston Film Festival, 1995.
- Award of Merit, House & Home magazine, research house project director, 1964.
- Award of Excellence for Record House, Architectural Record magazine, as project director for research house, 1964.

Books, Publications, Videos, Films

Books

Customer Service – the cornerstone of success, 2013, author, Gollywobbler Productions.

The Iron Indians, 2011, author, the story of the 1953 William & Mary football team, Gollywobbler Productions.

Communicating In A Crisis, 2008, author, Gollywobbler Productions.

Offsides! Fred Wyant's provocative look inside the NFL, author, 2001, Xlibris.

You'd Better Have A Hose If You Want to Put Out the Fire – the complete guide to crisis and risk communications, 2000, author, Gollywobbler Productions.

Bears Handbook - stories, stats and stuff about Baylor University Football, 1996, co-author with Michael Bishop, Midwest Sports Publishing.

Marketing Public Relations – the how's that make it work!, 1995, author, republished in paperback, 2000, Iowa State University Press and Wiley/Blackwell.

MIUS AND YOU - The Developer Looks at a New Utility Concept, 1980, co-author with Joseph Honick, Richard O'Neill and Fernando Oaxaca, U.S. Department of Housing and Urban Development, the first definitive book written on utility cogeneration.

How to Profitably Buy and Sell Land, 1977, author, John Wiley & Sons.

Vacation Homes Plans and Products Guide, 1965, editor, Hudson Publishing Co.

Contributor to the report of The President's Committee on Urban Housing (Kaiser Committee), 1968.

Contributor to the report of the National Commission on Urban Problems (Douglas Commission), 1967.

Screenplays

The Iron Indians, the story of the 1953 William & Mary football team, feature motion picture or movie for television, co-writer/producer with Gabor Nagy, registered 2011 with the Writers Guild of America, West.

Hot Rod, feature motion picture or movie for television with co-writer/producer Gabor Nagy about the life of Hot Rod Hundley, registered 2008 with the Writers Guild of America, West.

West Virginia Kid, feature motion picture or movie for television with co-writer/producer Gabor Nagy about the childhood life of Hot Rod Hundley, registered 2008 with Writers Guild of America, West.

Television and Video

George Bush Talks About His Presidential Library, 1995, 11-minute fund-raising video, executive producer and director, Bronze Medal, WorldFest Houston International Film Festival.

Clinton and Congress, 1995, one-hour bipartisan roundtable discussion of national issues at Texas A&M University, executive producer.

Marching to the Beat, half-hour television documentary about the history of marching bands, 1955, executive producer and writer, winner of the CINE Golden Eagle, the Oscar of non-theatrical production.

A Tribute to Achievement, half-hour documentary film of the 1984 U.S. Olympic Medal Winner's tour, executive producer and co-writer with Don Smith, winner of the CINE Golden Eagle, the Oscar of non-theatrical production.

Tone-Up for Tennis, 10-part syndicated television series on tennis tips starring Vic Braden, 1977, creator and executive producer.

The Jump Shot and *Individual Defensive Skills,* two 10-minute "how to" films starring Jerry West, Hot Rod Hundley and Pat Riley, created for Sunkist Growers, 1970, executive producer, creator, and writer.

Passing the Football and *Catching the Football,* two 10-minute "how to" football films starring John Brodie and Gene Washington, created for Sunkist Growers, 1972, producer, creator, and writer.

Special Publications

A Look at the U.S. Olympic Committee In 2000, co-author with David Jay Flood, the report of the USOC's Long Range Strategic Planning Task Force.

Overview of U.S. Cities and Livability, a white paper report for the U.S. Environmental Protection Agency, October 4, 1999.

A Corporate Management Compliance Assistance Guide – a primer on potential barriers to advancement, 1991, co-author with Jude Sotherlund, Office of Federal Contract Compliance Programs, U.S. Department of Labor.

Tone-Up for Tennis, 1977, author and creator, special publication for Armour-Dial in cooperation with the World Team Tennis league.

Enjoying Kings Hockey, 1975, author and creator, special publication for Alta-Dena Dairy and the Los Angeles Kings.

How to Play Basketball the Lakers Way, 1974, author and creator, special publication for Alta-Dena Dairy and the Los Angeles Lakers.

Bill Sharman's Basketball Tips, 1972, author and creator, series of five "how to" pamphlets created for Sunkist Growers and the Los Angeles Lakers.

The Care and Feeding of Superstars, 1971, author and creator, special publication about Jerry West for Sunkist Growers.

Index

3M 21, 33, 95, 96
7/Eleven 33
20th Century Fox 30, 87, 133
20th Century Limited 157
21 150, 160
1896 Olympic Games 153
1984 Olympic Games 29, 42, 88, 92, 173, 177
1988 Games in Seoul, Korea 40
1994 Cotton Bowl football game 50
1996 Olympic Games 43
Abbott & Costello 163
ABC-TV 41
Aberdeen Proving Ground, Md. 15
Academy of Television Arts and Sciences 48
Accardo, Tony (Big Tuna) 113
Acropolis 147, 153
Adelphia 73
Adelson, Merv 111, 112, 115, 116
adidas 29, 88
Adonis, Joe 113
affordable housing 38
AFTRA 34
Alabama 127
Aladdin 115
Alaska Airlines 165
Alberobello 153
Albright, Patsy 48
Aldrich, Robert 30
Alexandria. Va. 148
Alexis 19

Allan, Ingersoll, Segal & Henry 27, 175
Allen & Company 100
Allen, George 42
Allen, Marty 21
Allen, Mel 15
Allen, Rupert 32, 86
Allen, Steve 141
Alleva's 150
Al Queada 159
Alta-Dena Dairy 30, 63, 181
Altria tobacco 167
Alzheimer's 134, 140
Amalfi Coast 153
American Bar Association 79
American Builder magazine 111
American Eagle 94
American Song Festival 87, 88
American Tobacco Company 87
America's Cup 34, 135
America's Cup Festival of Sports 34
AMF Voit 30
Amherst College 165
Amherst, Lord Jeffrey 165
Amos 'n' Andy 163
Amsterdam 155, 156
Anchorage 156
Andrews, Julie 149
Anguilla 155
Ann Arbor, Michigan 113
An Officer and a Gentleman 112
Antoine's 157

Index | 183

Antwerp 138, 154
AOL/Time Warner 73
AP Parts 16
AP Stylebook 164
Arc de Triomphe 147, 154
Architectural Record
 magazine 178
Argentina 156
Argue, John 42, 88, 89, 92
Armour-Dial 181
Arnaud's 157
asbestos 38, 54
Ashcroft, Lord Michael 59, 60, 61
Asphalt Roofing Manufacturers'
 Association 23
Associated Press 79, 81, 164
Associated Press Stylebook 33
Association Générale des
 Fédérations Internationales de
 Sports 29
Astrodome 41
Athens 88, 136, 153
Atlantic City 87, 149
At Long Last Love 133
AT&T 72, 79, 167
Attica, New York Correctional
 Facility 127
AT&T Pebble Beach National Pro-
 Am Golf Tournament 35
Austin 45
Babe 30
Bache & Co. 24
Bache & Company 160
Bailey, Pearl 114
Baltimore Colts 8
Banks, Sam 8
Barbados 155, 161
Barcelona 156
Barnard 14
Barnes & Noble 50
Barnum, Phineas Taylor 87
Barone, Tony 48
Baron, Mark 88

Barrett, Eddie and Betty 158
Barrett, Edgar O. "Eddie" 11, 13
Barrow, Dean 61
Barry, Marion 147
basketball scandal 126
Bassano del Grappa 137
Bate, Terry and Janet 94
Baylor University Football 179
Baywatch 109
Beaman, Dean 35
Becket, MacDonald 39
Beekman Tower 150
Beijing 154
Being There 112
Belgium 131, 138, 154
believe in yourself 105
Belize 59, 61, 161
Belize Telecommunications 59, 61
Belize Telephone 70
Bell & Howell 8, 12
Bell, Jay 24, 25
Bell South 72, 79
Ben & Jerry 101
Berman, Bill 116
Berman, Charles M. 114
Berman, Jay 164
Bernays, Edward 87
Berra, Yogi 141
Better Business Bureau 82
Beverly Hills 27, 28, 134, 175
Beverly Wilshire Hotel 102
Bilingual Children's Television 28
Bing 161
Bing Crosby Clambake 35
Black Tie Garage Sale 134
Blackwell Sanders Peper
 Martin 75
Bogdanovich, Peter 133
Boise Cascade 116
Bollinger, Lee 76, 77
Bombay 154
Bonann, Gregory J. 109

184 | My Wonderful Life

Bonanno, Giuseppe (Joe Bananas) 113
Book of Kells 155
Bordeaux 154
Bosley, Bruce 13
Bowen, Ray 51
Bowling Green 127
Boyle, Patrick 54
Boy Scouts 4
Braden, Vic 180
Bradley, Tom 88, 89, 137
Brassart, Madam Élisabeth 135
Brasschaat 154
Breland, Mark 90
Brennan's 157
Breslin, Jimmy 16
Brewer, Gene C. 37
Brinkley, David 163
British Virgin Islands 59, 161
Broad, Eli 100, 116
Broadway 149
Brodie, John 180
Brooklyn Dodgers 144, 150
Brown 14
Browner, Carol 52, 54
Brown, Jerry 167
Brown, Robert N. "Red" 13
Brugge 154
Brussels 154
Bryan/College Station 147
Bryn Mawr 14
Buckingham Palace 154
Budapest 156
Buddhas of Bamiyan 166
budget management 120
Buenos Aires 156
build from within 32
Building Seismic Safety Council 39
Bunche, Ralph 114
Bundsen, Jerry 20
Bunn, Gary 12
Burnett, Carol 31, 67, 68, 102, 134

Burns, George 35
Burson, Harold 22, 23, 34
Burson-Marsteller 22, 34, 35, 43, 135
Bush, Barbara (Mrs. George H. W. Bush) 39
Bush, George H. W. 39, 136
Bush, George W. 52, 170
business dress 160
Byrnes, Jimmy 86
Cable & Wireless 73
Caen, Herb 20
Café Boulud 150
Caffé Florian 157
Cairo 153
California wine 22, 141
California Wine Institute 134
California Zephyr 157
Calleia, Anton 89, 137
Cambridge 177
Camel News Caravan 163
campaign strategy 46
Campbell, Bradley M. 52
Cannes 154, 164
Cape Breton 155
Cape Cod 155
Capital Airlines 157
Cap Juluca 155
Capone, Al (Scarface) 113
Cardenas, René 28
Caribbean 155, 161
Caribbean Broadcasting Union 78
Caribbean News Agency 78
Carlsbad 112
Carlson, Harry 33
Carlyle 150
Carmichael, Hoagy 133
Carnegie Deli 150
Carroll, Sherylon 47
Carter Ledyard & Milburn LLP 70
Casablanca 154
CBS 35, 102, 163
CBS-Klingbeil 116

Index | 185

Centex Corp. 116
Central Michigan 166
Century Plaza Hotel 41, 89
change In communicating 161
Charleroi, Pa. 2
Charleston Gazette 4, 12, 95
Charleston, W. Va. 1, 3, 5, 11, 95, 147, 157
Charlottetown 156
Chasen's 28, 157
Chevron 167
Chicago 157
Child, Julia 135
Chile 156
China 138
Chinatown 19, 151
Christiansted, St. Croix, U.S.V.I 58, 161
Christ the Redeemer 147
Christ the Redeemer Statue 156
Chumley's 150
Cincinnati Reds 163
CINE Golden Eagle 180
Cingular 79
clarinet 5
clarinet lessons 3
Clark, Susan 30
Cleveland, Detroit 113
Clinton, William J. 41, 180
Cobb salad 157
Coca-Cola 28, 100, 138
C&O Canal 148
Cock 'n Bull 28, 157
collateralized mortgage notes 24
College of Fellows 177
College of the Pacific 127
College of William & Mary 2, 6, 7, 11, 15, 65, 125, 167, 172, 175, 177, 178, 179
College Station, Texas 45, 176
Collier's 13
Colonial Williamsburg 7
Colosseum 147, 153

Columbia 14, 70, 75, 127
Columbia Journalism Review 69, 70, 71, 72, 73, 74, 75, 76, 77, 78, 79, 80
Columbia University 69, 75, 76, 80, 125, 126
Comcast 73
Commander's Palace 157
common courtesy 159, 160, 172
Common Glory 7
communication 121, 161
CONCACF 29
Confederation of North, Central American and Caribbean Associations of Football 29
Conference On Inflation 136
Connerly, Charlie 144
Connor, Dennis 135
Conrad, C. Carson "Casey" 30
Conteh, Dr. Abdulai 61
Conway, Tim 134
Copacabana 149
Copacabana Beach 156
Copain restaurant 125, 128, 129, 150
Copenhagen 155
Corinth Canal 153
Cornell 14
Costello, Frank 113
Council of Housing Producers 21, 22, 23, 84
Couric, Katie 102
Cousey, Bob 144
Cox, John 73, 167, 168
creative transportation 84
Creel, Col. George 143
criminal libel 80, 81
crisis and risk communications 179
Cronkite, Walter 102, 163
Crossen, Frank 116
Cruising 112
Cuba 113
Cub Scouts 4

186 | My Wonderful Life

Cullimore, Jack 97
customer service 52
Customer Service 178
Dahle, Karen 34
Dalitz, Morris B. "Moe" 112, 113, 114, 115, 116
Dallas 45, 112, 142
Dallas Cowboys 41
Dallas Morning News 49
Daniel 150
Danube River 156
Darling, Major General Thomas 85, 86
Dartmouth 14
Dassler, Adolph "Adi" 29
Dassler, Horst 28, 88
Davis, Jr., Sammy 103, 114, 149
D-Day 86
defamation 80, 81
Dektar, Cliff 33
Delaware 52
Desert Inn 112, 114
Desgrange, Henri 87
Diaz, Marta 47
Dilenschneider Group 70
Dilenschneider, Robert 70
Diller, Phyllis 20
Director's Guild 49
Disneyland 40, 152
Disneyworld 142
District of Columbia 52
Dixie Classic 140
document dates 120
Dolores Hidalgo, Mexico 173
Dominguez, Cari 43
Dominican Republic 73, 155
Dominique's 149
do-not-reply emails 172
Doro's 20
Draper, Don 160
dress code 160
Dreyfus Development 116
Drysdale, Don 23

Dubai 154
Dublin 155
Duffy's Tavern 163
Dukakis, Michael 40
Duke University 113
Duke Ziebert's 149
Dunes 115
Dylan, Bob 27
Eastabrook, Bill 96
Eastwood, Clint 35
Ebbets Field 150
Economic Policy Council on Rural Development 42
Eddie Condon's 150
Edelman, Daniel J. 21, 22, 23, 24, 57, 97, 175
Edgar Bergen & Charlie McCarthy 163
Ed Sullivan Show, The 16
Egypt 153
Eiffel Tower 147, 154
Eight Is Enough 112
Eisner, Michael 73
Eli Lilly 167
Ellis, Jan 43
El Paso 28
Elysée 150
Emmy 33, 48
Empire State Building 147, 150
Employment Retirement Income Security Act 24
English grammar 164
EPA 52, 102, 132
  news release distribution policy 53
Erickson, Dave 16
ERISA 24
Ernie's 19, 160
Eskimo 165
Essex House 150
establishing project timelines 47
Evans, William Dent "Bill" 12
Exley, Dot 16

Index | 187

Exley, Hazel 3
Exley, Lucius 3, 16
factory-built housing 38
Fairbanks, Alaska 156
Fairmont, The 20
Fairmont Times, The 12
Falcon Crest 112
Farmer's Home Administration 42, 176
Federal Election Commission 167
Fenway Park 171
Ferguson, Maynard 7
Fibber McGee & Molly 163
FIFA 29
fight back and win 63
 airline bureaucrats 68, 94
 Columbia Journalism Review 69
 federal bureucrats 65
 local bureaucrats 63, 66
 New York mayor's office 90
Filomena Ristorante 149
Finch, Robert H. 65
Finney, Jack 20
Fior d'Italia 19
First Amendment 50, 77, 167
Fisherman's Wharf 19
fixing basketball games 126
Flamingo 114
Fleming, Jack 12, 13
Flint, Michigan 54
Flood, David Jay 34, 181
Florida State 166
Flournoy & Gibbs 14, 16, 19, 175
follow-up file 118
Fonseca, Ralph 59, 60
Foolish Pleasure 106, 109
Football Writers Association of America 30
Ford, Betty (Mrs. Gerald) 35
Ford, Glenn 23, 134
Ford, President Gerald 35, 136
foreign influences 38
foreign languages 138, 139

Freedom of Information Act 48, 52, 54
Freeman, Jack 8, 9
Free Press, The 4
Friedman, Milton 139
Ft. Chaffee, Ark. 15
Ft. Hood, Texas 15
Ft. Wayne Zollner Pistons 126
Furfari, Mickey 12
Gage, Dr. E. Dean 45, 51
Galatoire's 157
Galleria Vittorio Emanuele II 153
Gannett Company 69, 74, 79
Garagiola, Joe 141
Gardner, Joedy 12
Garner, James 35
Garroway, Dave 163
gate guardians 99
 agents 102
 publicity flacks 102
General Association of International Sports Federations 88, 89
General Motors 101
Genovese, Vito (Don Vito) 113
George H. W. Bush Presidential Library and Museum 46, 50, 100, 180
Georgetown 148
Georgetown University Law School 177
George Washington 9
Getty, J. Paul 154
Ghiza 147
Gibbs, Katherine 14
Gibraltar 147
Gifford, Frank 143, 144
Giro di Italia 158
giving back 173
Giza 153
Glass Ceiling Initiative 43, 51, 169
Glenwood Landing, N.Y. 3, 132
Global Positioning System 107

Global Volunteers 173
GMA International 31
Godfather, The 128
Golden Gate Bridge 20
Golden Globe 33
Goldwyn Studios 33
golf 7
Gollywobbler Productions 176, 178, 179
González, Rep. Henry B. 39
Good Neighbor Sam 20
Goodwin, Doris Kearns 71
Goodwin, Richard N. 71
Google 73, 161
Gore, Al 170
Gotti, Roland 19
Gotti, Victor 19
Government Customer Service Improvement Act 172
Gozo 153
grammar 164
Granby High School 5, 158, 177
Grand Canyon 147, 152
Grand Central Oyster Bar 150
Grand Central Station 149
Grand Hyatt 150
Great Gildersleeve, The 163
Great Wall of China 147, 154
Greece 153
Greenbrier, The 12
Green Hornet, The 163
Green, Rep. S. William "Bill" 39
Green Valley, Ariz. 58, 147, 176
Greenwich Village 150
Griffith Stadium 148, 158
growing too quickly 32
GT&T 74
Guadeloupe 59, 155, 161
Guiding Light 163
Gumbel, Bryant 35
Gusoff, Bernard 128
Guyana Telephone & Telegraph 71, 73, 79

Haak, Dr. Al 9
Halifax 155
Hamilton, George 134
Hamilton, Joe 67, 134
Hardesty, David and Susan 158
Hardman, Shorty 4
Harry's Bar 153, 157
Harvard 14, 165
Harvard University Law School 177
Havana Conference 113
Hayworth, Rita 134
Head, Edith 21
Heinrich, Don 143, 144
Helmick, Bob 34
Helms, Sen. Jesse 42
Henri, Francois 2
Henry, Bruce 20, 57, 58, 131, 169
Henry, Deborah 20, 57, 58, 131, 169
Henry, Frank 2
Henry, Gillian Thompson 66
Henry, Marie Josephine Brichau 2
Henry, Rene 2
Hermitage, The 153
Hillcrest Country Club 89
Hill & Knowlton 33
Hilton 73, 88
Hirshorn 148
Hispanic marketing 28, 48, 171
Hitler, Adolph 131, 156
Hoffa, Jimmy 113, 114, 115
Hogan, Frank 126
Hollywood 16, 30, 40, 48, 133, 160
Holzman, Red 144
Homeland Security 159
Hong Kong 154
Honick, Joe 31, 96
Honor Code 9
Hope, Dolores (Mrs. Bob) 35
Horn and Hardart Automat 150
Hot Shoppes 149

Index | 189

House & Home magazine 31, 178
Houseman, John 93
Houston 45
Houston Galleria 41
Houston Oilers 41
how-to films 180
Hoyt, Michael 70, 71
Huff, Sam 12, 13
Hughes, Howard 114
Hundley, Rod (Hot Rod) 11, 13, 15, 140, 180
Hungry i 20
Hunter, Mark 69, 72, 73, 74, 75
Huntley, Chet 163
IBM 101, 162
ICC 74, 79
ICPR 28, 30, 31, 33, 49, 83, 86, 87, 88, 91, 102, 122, 152, 164, 171, 176
ICPR-West-Nally 89
Il Duomo 153
Indianapolis 500 16
indoor air quality 38
Ingersoll, Rick 25, 33, 102
Inner Sanctum 163
Innovative Communication Corporation 58, 59, 69, 70, 78, 93, 161, 176
inside the beltway 31, 37
Interagency Rural Development Strategy Task Force 42
Inter-American Development Bank 61
International Association of Fire Chiefs 95
International Brotherhood of Teamsters 113
International Olympic Committee 88, 136
International Velvet 30
Internet 161
IOC 88, 89, 136
Iowa State University Press 179

Ipanema Beach 156
Iron Indians, The 9
Isaacs, Neil D. 127
ISIS 159
ITT 69
Ivy Only 14
Jack Benny 163
Jacobson, Howard A. 75, 77
Jean-Pierre 149
Jensen, Dudley 7
Joe King's German-American Rathskeller 150
Joe's Special 19
Johnson, Rafer 142
Jones Beach 150
Jones, Bil 3
Jones, Jack 21
Jones, Jewell 3
Jones Printing Co. 4
Jucker, Ed 141
Julie & Julia 135
Julius' 150
Jumet 154
Jumpin' Branch, W. Va. 173
Jumpin' Frog Saloon 157
J.W. Marriott 150
Kalison, Pete 16
Kanawha Valley 1
Karras, Alex 30
Katzenbach, Rick 35
Kaufman & Broad 100, 116
keep copies 119
Keller, Tom 88, 89, 90
Kemp, Jack 41, 42
Kenton, Stan 7
Keough, Donald 28, 100
Kight, Howard 4
Killanin, Lord 136
Kimberly-Clark 141
Kingsfield On Contracts 93
Kingston Trio, The 20, 28
Kissinger, Henry 67, 68
Klingbeil, Jim 116

Knights of St. John 153, 178
Knokke-Heist 154
Knots Landing 112
Koch, Ed 91, 99, 142
Kodak 8
Korman, Harvey 134
Korn Ferry 51
Koskinen, John 116
Kountze, Tower 75
Kuhn, Bowie 42
La Chaumiere 149
La Cosa Nostra 113
La Costa 114, 115, 116
La Famiglia 28, 157
Lafayette, Indiana 133
Lakers 15, 34
Lamone, Gene "Beef" 12
Landia, Mark 88
Landor Associates 99, 100
land use guidelines 38
Lansky, Meyer 113
La Posta Vecchia 153
Larwin Group 116
LaSalle 127
La Scala 153
Lasorda, Tommy 103
Las Vegas 111, 112, 113, 114, 115
Lavery, Bea 137
lead-based paint 38
leadership 105
Leaders magazine 100
Le Cordon Bleu 135
Le Lion d'Or 149
Lemmon, Jack 23, 35
Lennar 116
Lennen & Newell 17, 20, 21, 118, 175
lesson in politics 42
Levine, Joseph E. 21
Levitt 116
Lewis and Clark 157
Lewis, Art "Pappy" 11
Lewiston, Idaho 114

libel 80, 81
Liberty 73
Liebert, Dick 149
Liege 154
Life magazine 13
Lincoln Park, N. J. 16
Linkletter, Art 23
Lisbon 155
Little Dix Bay 155
London 154
Lone Ranger 87, 163
Longest Yard, The 30
Longines Wittnauer 89
Long, Nate 49
Look 13
Lorimar Productions 112
Los Angeles 20, 21, 29, 34, 41, 66, 88, 89, 147, 157, 173, 175, 176, 177
Los Angeles City Council 177
Los Angeles Coliseum 171
Los Angeles County Board of Supervisors 177
Los Angeles County Health Department 30, 64
Los Angeles Dodgers 103
Los Angeles Kings 64, 181
Los Angeles Lakers 12, 24, 64, 140, 158, 181
Los Angeles Olympic Committee 34
Los Angeles Olympic Organizing Committee 173
Los Angeles Publicity Club 28, 178
Los Angeles Times 64, 92
Louie's 150
Luciano, Charles (Lucky) 113
Lucky Strike 87
Luft, Lorna 134
Lum and Abner 163
Lynch, John 151
Macco-Great Southwest 116

Index | 191

MacNamara, Julianne 142
Madison Avenue 13, 14
Madison Square Garden 15, 140, 141, 149, 151
Mad Men 14, 160
Magic Pan Restaurants 135
Major Bowes Amateur Hour 163
Make Room for Daddy 16
Malden, Karl 23
Malta 153
Ma Maison 157
Mamma Leone's 150
Mapp, Kenneth 74
Marchienne au Pont 154
marching bands 180
Marina Del Rey 106, 107, 108
Marin County 20, 21, 66
Mariner III 25
Marketing Public Relations 179
Marks, Michael 103
Marriott 73
Marriott East Side 150
Marshall, George C. 86
Martha's Vineyard 155
Martin, Dean 103, 149
Martinique 59, 155, 161
Martin, Mary 149
Maryland 52
Matera 153
MCA 113
McCabe, Michael 52, 53, 54
McCain-Feingold Campaign Reform Act 167
McCarthy, Frank 86
McCloskey, Anne 137
McCloskey, Robert 137
McFadden, Frank 33
McFadden, Strauss, Eddy & Irwin 27
MCI 72
McKay, Jim 13
McPherson Grill 149
McSorley's Old Ale House 150

Meany, George 136
Medill School of Journalism 5, 133
Meek, John 57
Melbourne, Australia 43
Memorial Day 54
memories 152
mentor young talent 32
Mexico 152
Mexico City 151
MGM 30, 33
Michaels-Stern 141
Midwest Sports Publishing 179
Mikan, George 15
Milan 153
Miller, Leonard 116
Minneapolis Lakers 15
Minnelli, Liza 134
Miss America Pageant 87
Mississippi College 166
MIUS 31
Mobley, Dr. William H. "Bill" 45, 49, 51
Modular Integrated Utility Systems 31
Mohawk Carpet 103
Molasky, Irwin 111, 112, 115, 116
Molinas, Jack 125, 126, 127, 128, 129
Monaco 155
Monday Night Football 30, 41
Montana 147
Monterey Peninsula Golf Foundation 35
Montevideo 156
Montreal 88
Montserrat 156
Mont-St.-Michel 154
Moomjian, Norman 125, 128
Moraga, Calif. 127
Morgantown Dominion-News 12
Morgantown, W. Va. 11, 14, 106, 140, 147, 175, 177
Morocco 138

192 | My Wonderful Life

Morse code 5
mortgage securities 24, 169
Mosher, John 148
Mosler, Edwin 143, 144
Mosler Safe Co. 143
Mountaineers 11, 12
Mount Holyoke 14
Movieola 12
Mt. Vernon, Va. 148, 152
Mt. Vesuvius 153
Muggs, J. Fred 163
Mumbai 154
Munroe Creative Partners 97
Munroe, Judy 97
Murdoch, Rupert 73
Murrow, Edward R. 163
Musa, Said 59, 60, 61
Mycenae 153
My Fair Lady 149
my favorite places 147
Nagy, Gabor 25, 179, 180
Nally, Patrick 28, 29, 88, 96
Nantucket 155
National Association of Home Builders 37
National Basketball Association 125
National Collegiate Athletic Association 45, 166
National Commission on Urban Problems 179
National Endowment for the Arts 48
National Endowment for the Humanities 48
National Enquirer 67, 68
National Homes 116
National Homes Corporation 68, 133
National Institute of Building Sciences 37, 38, 39, 41, 176
Native Americans 166
Navstar 107

Navy 9, 15
Nazi 131, 132, 156
NBC 34, 35, 102, 137
NCAA 126
N.C. State 127
Nedick's 150
Nelson, Ozzie and Harriett 23
Netherlands, The 138
New Brunswick 156
New Orleans 157
Newport News Daily Press 11
News Corp. 73
new technology 162
new world 159
New York 13, 14, 15, 19, 33, 34, 57, 83, 87, 125, 132, 142, 145, 147, 149, 151
New York Baseball Writers' Association 144
New York Central Railroad 3, 5
New York Giants 16, 143, 144, 150
New York Hilton 150
New York Knicks 15, 144, 158
New York Society of Security Analysts 22
New York Times 14
New York University 127, 140
New York World's Fair 150
New York Yankees 126, 150
Niagara Falls 147
Nice 154
Nichols, Erna 173
Nicklaus, Jack 35
Nick's 150
NIT 126
Nixon, Richard M. 65, 143, 144
Nordstrom, Bruce 101
Norfolk Tars 5
Norfolk, Va. 5, 39, 147, 177
Normandy 154
Normandy Invasion 86
North Beach 19
North Carolina 6, 127

North Carolina State 9
North Dakota 147
Northwestern University 133
Notre Dame 15
Novak, Kim 21
Nova Scotia 155
Oaxaca, Fernando 28, 31
Occidental Petroleum 167
O'Connor, Ray 34, 135
Office of Management and Budget 28
office procedure 47
Ohio State 111
Ohlmeyer, Don 35
Oklahoma 149
Oklahoma State 51
Olympic Games 29, 34, 89, 90, 136
Olympic medal women's tour 142
Olympic sports 33
Olympic stadiums 158
Omaha, Nebraska 69
O'Meara, Mark 35
O'Neill, Richard 31, 179
Order of St. John of Jerusalem 178
organized crime 113
organize for success 117
Oriental Pearl 151
Orlando, Fla. 142
Oscar 33, 48, 87
Ostuni, Italy 153, 173
O'Toole, Peter 87
Owens-Corning 14, 17
Oxford 165
PAC 166, 167
Pacific Northwest 161
Paige, Erik 5, 6
Palace Hotel 19
Palmer, Richard 89
Palm Springs 33
Palos Verdes 66
Panama Canal 157
Paper Chase 93

Paper Mate Pens 141
Paradise Development Co. 112
Paramount Pictures 21
Paris 27, 135, 154
Parmele, Gil 16
Parthenon 147, 153
Paschall, Dr. Davis Y. 65, 66
Patton 86
Pearl Harbor 131
Pebble Beach Company 35
penguins 158
Penn 14
Penn Station 149
Pennsylvania 52
pension fund investments 169
Penthouse magazine 115
Perenchio, Jerry 23, 96
Perl-Mack 116
PERT chart 123
Perth, Australia 34, 135
Peters, Tom 101
Philadelphia 51, 55, 57, 97, 132, 147, 176
Picasso Madura Gallery 154
Pierre 150
Pillsbury Bake-Off 87
Pittsburgh Pirates 144
Pittsburgh Press 54
P.J. Clarke's 150
planting misinformation 91
Playboy Mansion 30
Plaza Athénée 150
Plaza Hotel 84, 142, 150
Political Action Committees 166
political correctness 165
Polo Grounds 144, 150
Pompeii 153
Porter, Cole 133
Portia Faces Life 163
Posert, Harvey 21, 22
Premier of Western Australia 34
Preminger, Otto 21

194 | My Wonderful Life

presidential election campaign 39, 176
Presidential Fitness Award 30
President's Council on Physical Fitness and Sports 30, 143
Price, David 116
Price, Jim 133
Price, Vincent 23
Primack, Sam 116
Prima, Louis 7
Prince, Bob 144
Prince Edward Island 156
Princess Anne Country Club 7
Princeton 14
Prine, Malcolm 116
Prior, Cornelius 74
Prosser, Jeffrey J. 58, 60, 69, 70, 71, 72, 74, 76, 77, 78, 79, 80, 161
Proxmire, Sen. William 39
PRSA Silver Anvils 178
Public Relations Man of the Year 21, 178
Public Relations Society of America 27, 28, 177, 178
Public Relations Society of Texas 178
Puck, Wolfgang 157
Puerto Madryn 158
Puerto Montt 156
Puerto Rico 81, 155
Punta Arenas 156
Punta Tombo 158
Purple Onion 20
Qantas 135
Quaker Oats 141
Quayle, Dan 39
Quill & Scroll Society 5, 133
Qwest 72
Radcliffe 14
radio 162
Radio City Music Hall 149
radon 38
Raleigh, N.C. 140

Ramphal, Sir Shridath "Sonny" 59
Ramsay, Sir Bertram 86
Rancho La Costa Resort & Spa 112, 114, 115
Rangoon 154
raw-certified milk 30
Reagan, Ronald 142
recruit at the entry level 32
recycled paper 53, 170
Redmond, Wash. 58
Red Skelton 163
Reich, Ken 92
Rene A. Henry Co. 176
Rene A. Henry, Inc. 23, 175
Republican Governors Conference 133
Republican National Convention 40
Requests for Proposal 31
Resorts International Hotel in Atlantic City 103
Retton, Mary Lou 142
Reveal, Clara Bell Jarret 2
Reveal, C. O. 2
Reykjavik, Iceland 153
RFP 31
Rhodes, Cecil 165
Richardson, Elliot 65
Rich, Buddy 7
Richmond 9
Richter 73, 75
Rieger, Hank 137
Ries, Marshall 8, 16
Riley, Pat 180
Ringling Bros. and Barnum & Bailey Circus 87
Rio de Janeiro 156
Rive Gauche 149
Roberts, John 166
Robertson, Marsha 33
Robertson, Oscar 141
Rockefeller Center 149, 150
Rockettes 149

Index | 195

Roen, Allard 112, 113, 114, 115
Rogers & Cowen 33
Rogers, Wayne 35
Rohn, Lee 74
Rome 153
Romney, George 24
Roosevelt, Franklin Delano 160
Roosevelt, John 160
Roosevelt Junior High School 4
Rose Bowl 158, 171
Rosen, Charley 126
Rossi, Steve 21
Royal Bank of Trinidad & Tobago 60
Rumbaugh, Stanley 35
Rutenberg, Charles 116
Ruth, Stephen G. 86
Ryan Homes 116
SAG 34
Sahl, Mort 20
Saint-Martin 59, 155, 161
Sakazaki, Jack 29, 89, 96
salmonella 30, 64
Salt Lake City 57
Saltman, Shelly 23, 96
San Angel Inn 152
San Anselmo 66
San Antonio 28
Sanders, Sir Ronald Michael 59, 78, 80
San Diego 112, 115
San Diego Chargers 35
San Francisco 9, 16, 19, 20, 21, 28, 58, 95, 100, 147, 152, 157, 160
San Francisco Bay Area Publicity Club 21, 178
San Francisco Chronicle 20, 128
San Juan 94
Sans Souci 149
Santa Monica 107
Santa Monica Bay 106, 107
Santa Monica Evening News 169
Santayana, George 166
Santiago, Chile 139, 156
Sarajevo, Yugoslavia 137
Sardi's 150
Sarkowsky, Herman 116
Scandia 28, 157
Scarmado, Lillian Fickey 48
Schaus, Fred 11, 34
Schneider, Roy 74
Schrafft's 150
Schroeder's 20
Schwarzenegger, Arnold 40
Scott, George C. 35
Scott, Lester 15, 151
Scott, Mark 5
Seattle 20, 58, 147, 161, 176
Seattle World's Fair 9
secondary mortgage market 24, 169
Secrest, Lillian Henry 39
Secrest, Pop 3, 7, 163
Secrest, William K. 3, 5, 39
Segal, Mort 32, 33, 102
Seiko 89, 90
semaphore 5
Senate Foreign Relations Committee 42
Senate Labor Committee 24
Señor Pico 157
Seton Hall 127, 141
Seven Sisters 14
Shadow, The 163
Shanghai 154
Shepard, Ira Michael 24
Shepherd, Cybil 133
Sheraton 73
Sheridan, Ind. 2
Shor, Toots 90
Sigma Nu 8
Silver Anvils 27, 28
Silver Spurs 178
Simon, Bill 91
Simpson Timber Company 17, 20, 58, 111

Sinatra, Frank 103, 113, 149
Singapore Sling 157
Sint Maarten 59, 94, 155, 161
Slater, Frankie Lee 33
Slocum, R. C. 48
Smith, Don 33, 90, 96, 99, 142, 143, 180
Smith, Herman J. 37, 39
Smith, Jack 101
Smithsonian 148
Smothers Brothers 20
Smurfs 32
Snake River 157
Society of Professional Journalists 79
Solters, Lee 103
Sotherlund, Jude 43, 58, 181
Sound of Music, The 149
South Africa 165
South Charleston, W. Va. 2, 4
South Dakota 147
Southern Conference 11
Southfork Ranch 142
Southland Corporation-7/Eleven 33, 90, 93, 143
Spa 154
Spanish Steps 153
Spanos, Alex 35
special events 87
Sphinx 147, 153
Sport Accord 29, 88
Sport Billy 32
Sports Illustrated 13
sports information director 8, 9, 11, 12
sports marketing 24, 28, 30, 171
Sprint 79
Stanfill, Dennis 134
Stanfill, Terry 134
Stardust 114
Staten Island 149
stay the course 106
St. Croix Source 74

St. Croix, U.S.V.I. 59, 93, 155, 161, 176
Stephenson, Lane 47, 48
Stern, Bill 163
St. Francis Hotel 19
St. James Theatre 149
St. John 155
St. John, Jill 21
St. John's 127
St. Joseph's of Philadelphia 127
St. Jude's Hospital 16
St. Mark's Square 153, 157
St. Mary's College 127
St. Moritz 150
Stonehenge 154
Stone, Robert J. "Bob" 22
Stony Brook, N. Y. 16
St. Petersburg, Russia 153
Straeter, Ted 7
Strauss, John 27, 32, 33
Street, Timothy 35
St. Regis 150
St. Thomas 155
St. Thomas Source 74
St. Thomas, U.S.V.I. 59
Studio 54 150
Stueve, Harold J. J. 64
Stunt Man 87
stunts 87
Stuyvesant High School 126
Stylebook 164
Sugarloaf Mountain 147, 156
Sunkist 21, 23, 24, 141, 180
Sunkist Growers 181
Supreme Court 166, 167, 171
Surf Club 7
Swayze, John Cameron 163
Swiss Timing 88, 89, 90
Sydney, Australia 135
Taliban 159, 166
Teamsters Pension Fund 114
telephone log 118

Index | 197

Television for All Children
  (TVAC) 49
telling it like it is 85
tennis tips 180
Terra Cotta Warriors 147, 154
Terrail, Patrick 157
terror groups 159
Texas 147
Texas A&M University 44, 45, 46,
  47, 49, 50, 53, 85, 100, 122, 123,
  176
  A&M System 51
  Corps of Cadets 45, 50, 85
  crises
    Brazos County Grand Jury 49
  Fightin' Texas Aggie Band 50, 86
  political cartoon 50
  student newspaper 50
Texas Tech University 46
Thames, The 154
The Iron Indians 178, 179
The President's Committee on
  Urban Housing 179
Thomas, Danny 16
Thompson, Gillian 16
Thomson, Bobby 144
Thorpe, Jim 35
Three Gorges Dam 154
Tierra del Fuego 157
Tilden, Brad 165
Time 13
time management 122
time sheets 47
Times Square 149
Timex 90
Title IX 170
Tivoli Gardens 155
Tobacco States Football Network 5
Today Show 35, 163
to do list 118
Tokyo 154
Toledo, Ohio 16, 17, 19, 147, 175
Tonga Room 20

Tonight Show, The 141
Toomey, Bill 28, 96
Toots Shor's 16, 150
Top of the Mark 20
Torme, Mel 7
Tortola 155
Tour de France 87
Tournament of Champions 114
Trevi Fountain 153
Trinidad & Tobago 155, 161
turfs in higher education 48
Turin 153
turning down business 32
typing 4
UCLA 111
Ueberroth, Peter 35, 89, 90, 92
UNESCO 78, 158
United Dye and Chemical
  Corporation 114
United Nations 29, 150
United Press 6
University of California -
  Berkeley 28, 29, 139
University of Cape Town 165
University of Chicago 139
University of Cincinnati 141
University of Houston 46
University of Pittsburgh 145
University of Southern
  California 164
University of Texas 46
University of Virginia 30
UPI 6
Uruguay 156
U.S. Agency for International
  Development 42, 176
U.S. Army 15
U.S. Army induction 4
U.S. construction industry 38
U.S. Department of Agriculture 42,
  176
U.S. Department of Health,
  Education & Welfare 24, 65, 66

U.S. Department of Housing &
  Urban Development 24, 31, 41,
  179
U.S. Department of Interior 54
U.S. Department of Justice 53, 54,
  114
U.S. Department of Labor 43, 51,
  148, 176, 181
U.S. Environmental Protection
  Agency 51, 53, 170, 176, 181
  news release distribution
    policy 53
  transparency policy 54
U.S. Home 116
Ushuaia 156
using sports to sell the message 46
U.S. Military Academy 15, 143,
  151, 175
USO 149
U.S. Olympians 142
U.S. Olympic Committee 34, 91,
  150, 173, 181
U.S. Olympic Medal Winner's
  tour 180
U.S. Olympic Team 40
U.S. Overseas Private Investment
  Corporation 61
U.S. Plywood Corp. 37
U.S. Postal Service 164
U.S. Soccer Federation 29
U.S. Virgin Islands 58, 74, 81
Utah 127, 166
Utah Jazz 140
utility cogeneration 179
Valley Forge National Park 54
Valparaiso, Chile 156, 158
Vancouver, B.C. 155
Vano, Tom 96
Van Vechten, Sharon 84
Vassar 14
Vatican City 153
Venice 107, 153
Venice Beach 108, 109

Verizon 72, 73, 79
Via Condotti 153
video news releases 12, 13
Vienna 156
Villa Alegre 28
Viña del Mar 156
Virginia 5, 6, 52
Virginia Beach, Va. 6, 7, 147
Virginia Tech 9
Virgin Islands Daily News 58, 69,
  71, 75, 79, 80
Virgin Islands Telephone
  Company 69
Vitelco 74
VMI 86
Vondras, John 59, 60
Wachau Valley 157
Wake Forest 9, 140
Waldorf Astoria 150
Wall Street 160
Wall Street Journal 70
Walmart 167
Walsh, John J. 70, 71, 76, 77
Waltons 112
Warwick 150
Washington 57
Washington, D.C. 36, 37, 142, 147,
  161, 176, 177
Washington, Gene 180
Washington Monument 147, 148
Washington Senators 148, 158
Wasserman, Lew 113
Watt, Ray 116
WCBS-TV 13
Weaver, Robert C. 41
Weinberg, Larry 116
Weissman/Markovitz 33
Weissman, Murray 33, 87
Wellesley 14
Wells Fargo 87
Werbelin, Sonny 91
Westbrook, Peter 90
Western Union 5

Index | 199

West, Jerry 12, 24, 140, 158, 180, 181
Westminster Abbey 154
West-Nally 28, 88, 89
West Palm Beach, Fla. 147, 161, 176
West Point 15, 16, 143, 151, 175
West Virginia 52
West Virginia University 9, 11, 34, 140, 144, 158, 172, 175, 177
Whirlpool 33
Whirlpool Corp. 28
White, Betty 23
White Castle 149
White House 136
White House Personnel Office 41, 42
White, Pete 12
White Sulphur Springs 12
Wikipedia 12, 161
Wilde, Cornel 21
William & Mary, College of, 2, 6, 7, 11, 15, 65, 125, 167, 172, 175, 177, 178, 179
Williams, Andy 23, 35
Williamsburg, Va. 6, 175, 177
Williams, Paul 87
Williams, Robert G. 17, 20, 21, 118, 119
Williams, Russell 5
Wilson, Woodrow 165
Wine Institute 22
wine tasting events 23
Wisniewski, William "Bill" 53
Witting, Paul 12
WNOR 5
Wolper, David 137
Women In Communication 177
World Bank 61
World Cup 29, 90
World Cycling Championships 137
world famous wineries 154
WorldFest Houston Film Festival 178, 180
World Gymnastics Championships 156
World Institute of Black Communications 178
World Trade Center 132
World Trade Organization 78
World War II 131
Wright, Frank Lloyd 68
Wrigley Field 171
Writers Guild of America, West 179, 180
Wyant, Fred 12, 179
Xi'an, China 173
Yahoo 73
Yale 14
Yangon 154
Yangtze River 157
Yankee Stadium 150
Yoplait 101
Young & Rubicam 35
Your Hit Parade 163
Zabar's 150
Zaharias, Babe Didrikson 30
Zick, Timothy 167
Ziffren, Paul 89

Table of Contents

Chapter 1:   How It All Began 1
Chapter 2:   Returning Home To West Virginia 11
Chapter 3:   Open Your Golden Gates 19
Chapter 4:   Changing Times 27
Chapter 5:   Inside The Beltway 37
Chapter 6:   Deep In The Heart Of Texas 45
Chapter 7:   A Taste Of Retirement 57
Chapter 8:   You Can Fight Back And Win 63
Chapter 9:   Creativity On Demand 83
Chapter 10: Gate Guardians 99
Chapter 11: Always Believe In Yourself 105
Chapter 12: Breakfast With The Godfather 111
Chapter 13: Organize For Success 117
Chapter 14: How Mo Mo Saved My Life 125
Chapter 15: Memorable Moments 131
Chapter 16: Some Of My Favorite Places 147
Chapter 17: A New World 159
             Epilogue 169
             Appendix 175
             Index 183

Other Books by Rene A. Henry

Customer Service: the cornerstone of success, Gollywobbler Productions, 2013

The Iron Indians, the story of the incredible 1953 William & Mary football team, Gollywobbler Productions, 2011

Communicating In A Crisis, a guide for management, Gollywobbler Productions, 2008

Offsides! Fred Wyant's Provocative Look Inside the National Football League, Gollywobbler Productions and Xlibris, 2001

You'd Better Have A Hose If You Want To Put Out the Fire, the complete guide to crisis and risk communications, Gollywobbler Productions, 2001

Bears Handbook – Stories, Stats and Stuff About Baylor University Football, co-author with Mike Bishop, Midwest Sports Publishing, 1996

Marketing Public Relations – the HOWs that make it work!, Iowa State University Press/Blackwell Wiley Publishing, hardcover 1995, paperback 2000

MIUS and You – The Developer Looks At A New Utility Concept, co-author with Joseph J. Honick, Fernando Oaxaca and Richard O'Neill, U.S. Department of Housing & Urban Development, 1980

How To Profitably Buy & Sell Land, John Wiley & Sons, 1997